DON'T
RIFF-F

C000098443

©Anne Fothergill 2014

ISBN: 978-1-907257-77-3

This is a work of non-fiction based on the experiences and recollections of the author. Names have been changed to protect the privacy of individuals.

Published in 2014 by
Quoin Publishing Ltd.
17 North Street, Middlesbrough,
England. TS2 1JP

"For a woman brought up by nuns this is an incredibly gritty and frank account of life in a 1960s boarding house inhabited by those on the fringes of society. It is a book full of outrageous and colourful characters who leap off the page as well as hilarious anecdotes, beautifully told. Readers will be reduced to both tears of laughter and sadness as Anne embraces her new found freedom but is ultimately enriched by the people she meets, as she enriches them."

Victoria Williams
North News

Downstairs Nursery, Nazareth House - Anne aged fifteen is pictured on the far right.

The only remaining picture of Anne's mother.

Contents

THE ARRIVAL

It's better than those other doss houses,' Katie says as she rings the doorbell.

We are standing on the doorstep of a three storey Victorian house.

'It's definitely an improvement,' I reply.

Through the glass door we see a figure emerging into the hallway. There's a jangling of keys and eventually the door opens and a little old woman wearing an apron appears.

'What do you want?' she asks.

'We have come about the bedsit,' Katie says.

The old woman is suspicious. She eyes us up and down. 'Are there just the two of you?'

'Yes,' I say.

'Wait here,' she replies.

She goes back inside and closes the door. When she comes out again she is holding a bunch of keys. She locks the door and puts them in a pocket of her apron.

'The bedsit is next door,' she says.

We follow her down the long path. She shuts her garden gate and double checks that the latch is fastened. This woman is very security conscious, I think. We go round to the house next door.

I'm disappointed. Unlike her house this one is quite dingy looking. There is a large crack in the bay window and the paint is peeling off the door and framework.

She puts a key in the door expecting it to be locked, but it isn't.

1

'How many times have I told them to keep the front door locked?' she says.

She opens the door and we follow her inside.

We pass a room on the right and there are others along the hallway but she makes for the staircase. She goes up the stairs, leaning heavily on the banister and stopping every so often to complain that her knees are killing her.

'I'm too old for this,' she grumbles.

We hear music. The record *Paint it Black* by the *Rolling Stones* is playing.

'Aw, hope he's not down in the dumps again,' the old woman says. 'We can't go through that again.'

I wonder who she is referring to. I look at Katie and she shrugs her shoulders.

We arrive on the second floor and thankfully for the old woman this is where the bedsit is. She stops at a room with the number six on the door. She fumbles with her bunch of keys, picks one out and unlocks the door. It opens into a dark, gloomy bedsit.

We go inside and the room reeks of stale cigarettes. She goes over to the window and draws back orange curtains. It sheds light on the green patterned wallpaper so fashionable in the sixties. There are two single beds with faded yellow quilted bedspreads, a little stove, a sink, two chairs and a table with an ashtray on it. An old well-worn arm chair is in the corner of the room. But, overall, I'm happy with what I see.

The old woman is impatient. 'Well then, do you want it or not?' she snaps.

2

'Er, yes, I think so,' I say, trying not to sound too keen. Katie has warned me they might put the rent up if they know we are desperate. The truth is it is late afternoon and we have nowhere else to go.

'I'll want paying today and then you can pay me weekly,' she says.

Katie hands her the rent money. The old woman turns the coins over in her hands and when satisfied she puts them in her pocket.

'I've had a few dodgy ones,' she says. 'I have to check it.'

She goes out of the bedsit and we hear her knocking on the door of one of the other rooms.

'Tania, are you there?' she asks.

We hear a muffled reply, then a door opening.

'I've paid me rent this week,' we hear someone say.

'I know you have. I just want you to come to my house and get a rent book for the new tenants in number six,' the old woman replies.

Why doesn't she just ask *us* to come and get it, I think, does she not trust us?

The old woman returns to our room and she hands Katie two keys.

'That's the one for your room and that's the one for the front door. Tania will bring you the rent book. Don't forget to lock the front door on your way in and out. I don't want any riffraff coming into any of my houses,' she says.

The music has grown louder. It's coming from the floor above us.

Black as night, black as coal, the distinctive voice of Mick Jagger cries out.

The old woman stops, listens awhile and then slowly makes her way down the stairs.

Katie shuts the door. I stretch myself out on one of the beds.

'Ah, this is great, at last we've found somewhere decent,' I say.

But Katie disagrees. 'It's a dump,' she says, 'but it'll do for now. It's not as cheap as the other places, but that last one we looked at was a dive.'

'I wouldn't trust that landlord either,' I say, 'he was creepy, wasn't he? 'I'm available night and day if you want me,' he said. Yeah, I thought, I bet you are. I didn't like the way he said it.'

'I couldn't get out of the place fast enough,' Katie says, 'and it stunk an' all.'

There is a knock on the door and I jump up to open it. It's a young lass who looks about our age. She has a beehive and is all dolled up in a mini skirt, kohl eyeliner and pink lipstick.

'Hi, I'm Tania,' she says. 'I live at number four. So, you are the new tenants? Welcome to the Den of Iniquity.'

She sees that we are concerned. She grins.

'Well, that's what we tenants call it,' she says as she walks into the room and puts the rent book on the table.

'Mrs Lowe has asked me to give you the rent book. She likes to be paid every Thursday. She won't handle money on a Friday. It's against her religion. She's Jewish, you know,' Tania tells us.

'Mrs Lowe, is that her name?' I ask.

4

'Yes, she's the landlady. She owns both this house and the one next door. She lives alone now, her husband died ages ago. They reckon she's loaded,' Tania says.

'She's got bad knees,' I say. 'She struggled to get up the stairs.'

'Ah, she can pile it on can Mrs Lowe for the sympathy but believe me, if you miss the rent she'll come running up them stairs. She's frightened you'll do a bunk,' Tania replies.

'Have many people done that?' Katie asks.

'Yeah, loads,' Tania says. She looks around. 'It's not a bad room this,' she adds, 'I wouldn't have minded it meself. But I need to have a back room so I can look out for my clients when they call.'

What clients? Does she run some sort of business?

'Who put you on to this place?' she asks.

'We found it advertised in a shop window down the road,' I say.

Katie goes over to the stove and rattles the kettle. 'I'm dying for a cuppa,' she says.

She looks in the tea caddy, but there are hardly any tealeaves left. 'We'll have to get some matches to light the stove,' she says.

'We need to get some milk,' I add. 'I don't like black tea.'

'Why don't you come to my bedsit and I'll make you a cuppa,' Tania says.

We thank her.

'Don't forget to lock your door every time you leave,' she warns, 'there's thieves about. I can't guarantee that'll work, but it makes it just that bit harder for 'em.

'And don't lose your keys, Mrs Lowe charges a fortune to get another set made.'

Katie locks the door and we follow Tania to her room. Upstairs, the record has been changed. It's Dusty Springfield's *I don't know just what to do with myself.*

'Bloody heck,' Tania says, 'I'll have to pop up later and see how he is. The boyfriend's away and he's suicidal.'

Suicidal? Katie and I are shocked. Tania puts the key in the lock and flings open the door. 'Come in,' she says, 'I'll just put the kettle on.' She goes over to a tiny stove, fills the kettle from a tap in the sink and plonks it on the gas stove. She strikes a match, puts it under the kettle and a blue flame ignites.

We look around the bedsit. It's smaller than ours and there's not much room to sit down. Frilly bras and undies are drying on a clotheshorse near a one bar electric fire and pantyhose are slung over the back of a chair.

'Sit here,' she says as she removes magazines from her bed and puts them underneath.

It's a double bed covered with a soft tiger print blanket. The bed is near the window and overlooks the back garden. I look out and see that there is a path leading to the back door. The garden is a mess, though, overgrown with weeds. 'That's a big garden,' I say.

'Ah, the *rose garden* we call it,' Tania laughs.

A rose garden and not one bloom in sight, I'm thinking.

6

'It might have been one decades ago,' Tania says, 'but it ain't one now. Mrs Lowe keeps saying she is going to restore it back to its former glory but she says that every year. She won't fork out the money.'

She goes over to a small cabinet attached to the wall and takes down three cups. She places a small tea strainer over one cup and then puts a teaspoon of tealeaves into it. She lifts a carton of milk out of the sink and smells it.

'Oh bugger, the milk's gone off,' she says. I offer to go and get some.

'I know where the shop is,' I tell her. 'It's the same shop where we saw the advert for the bedsit.' Tania hands me half a crown. 'I won't be long,' I say. I'm feeling quite content now that we have found somewhere to stay.

FAYE

I start making my way down the stairs. There's a man sitting on the bottom step. He has dark cropped hair and is smoking a cigarette.

He turns around when he hears me coming. I'm taken aback. It's not a man, it's a woman, but why is she wearing a man's suit and tie?

She stands up but seems unsteady on her feet. I think she's drunk.

She gives a wolf whistle. 'Fucking 'ell!' she says. 'You're gorgeous.'

Is she talking to me? I look behind but there's no one else around. I don't know what to make of her. I've never had another woman make a pass at me before. *Whatever would the nuns say?*

'What you doing here?' she asks.

I should tell her to mind her own business, I think, but I'd better not as she looks quite intimidating.

'We've just moved in, me and my friend,' I tell her.

'What bedsit are you in?' she asks.

I worry she might come knocking on our door if I am honest, but I need to get to the shop.

'It's on the second floor,' I say.

She grins. 'You're next door to me and Jo,' she says.

Oh no, I think.

'You've got Lackey's bedsit. He got nicked, he's in Strangeways,' she tells me.

'Strangeways?' I ask.

'It's a prison, didn't you know?' she says.

'No, I'm not from round here. We just arrived in Manchester today,' I tell her.

'Didn't think you were,' she replies. 'Where are you from?'

'The North East,' I say.

'Where's that?' she asks.

'In the North East,' I reply.

'Are you taking the piss?' she asks.

'No, I'm not,' I say.

'You don't sound like a Geordie,' she says.

'I'm not from Newcastle,' I tell her.

'Where are you from?' she is asking.

'Erm, Robin Hoods Bay,' I lie.

'That's Nottingham, isn't it?' she says.

It's actually nearer to Whitby, but I won't tell her that.

I edge further down the stairs as she's coming up. She nearly loses her balance and grabs hold of the banister. She stops on the step below me.

'I were nearly a gonna there,' she chuckles. She steadies herself.

'Did Mrs Lowe show you round? The landlady?' she asks.

'Yes,' I say.

'She's OK, is Mrs Lowe,' she laughs, 'as long as you pay the rent. Where are you going?'

'I'm going to the shop for some milk,' I tell her.

'Come and 'ave a cup of char with me and Jo,' she says.

'No, thank you,' I say politely.

'Ah well, do us a favour and get us some ciggies,' she says.

I get the feeling she is used to giving orders and getting her own way. Not one to cross, I think.

'I don't have enough money,' I tell her.

'Here, I'll give you a quid. Get us twenty Players Number Six.'

She fumbles in her pocket and takes out a crumpled pound note. A strong whiff of alcohol wafts over me as she hands me the money. Reluctantly, I take it.

'I live at number five,' she says.

Now, she's blocking my way.

'Excuse me,' I say.

She staggers back against the wall to let me pass. I'm concerned.

'You need to hold on to the banister, you might fall down the stairs,' I tell her.

Dark eyes glare at me. I think she is going to hit me but she grins, 'I'll be OK, don't worry about me.'

I can feel her eyes boring into the back of my neck as I move down the stairs.

I'm just about to reach the bottom step when she shouts, 'I like you! What's your name, darlin'?'

I turn round. 'I'm called Anne,' I say.

'Thought you'd be called Marilyn. You look like a film star,' she says.

'Oh, I'm named after a saint,' I say. I'm grinning as I walk on down the hallway.

'You've come to the right place, darlin'', she says as she gives a throaty laugh. 'This is the Den of Iniquity.'

THE RAID

It felt really weird getting into an unfamiliar bed. The mattress was lumpy and there was an old kind of smell to it. I was nearest the light switch so I got up and turned it off. The street lamp shone through the opening in the curtains as they didn't quite join together. Katie and I lay in our single beds in semi darkness. We could hear music coming from the upstairs bedsit.

'When you were out at the shops,' Katie said, 'Tania told me that a lad called Liam lives upstairs. He tried to kill himself. Swallowed a load of pills, he did. The other tenants try to keep an eye on him. Apparently, they know what mood he's in just by the records he's playing. Tania says they listen out for them.'

'How strange,' I replied.

'Tania's concerned about him because his boyfriend's in the nick and he's having one of his downers. She said he's queer.'

'Does that mean he's weird?'

'No, they call him queer because he likes other men.'

'What do you mean he likes other men?' I asked, confused.

'He has sex with them.'

'What! How does a man have sex with another man?'

'Dunno. If we get to know him you could ask.'

'No way. I wouldn't dare.'

I thought over what she'd said. I was shocked.

The nuns in the orphanage had never discussed sex between a man and a woman never mind two men. *Crikey!*

'You should have seen that woman on the stairs,' I said. 'She was dressed like a man. She made a pass at me an' all. I tell you it's one weird place, is this. She asked me to get her a packet of cigarettes and when I brought them to her room she didn't even answer. Tania says she'll have probably passed out with the drink.'

'That Tania,' Katie replied lowering her voice, 'I'm sure she's on the game.'

'What does that mean?'

'She's a prostitute.'

'Never, she seems really nice.'

'That's what she meant by her clients calling,' Katie said. 'Bet she sneaks 'em in the back door.'

'I hope they don't come knocking on our door. I'll tell them where to go.'

'As soon as we get some money together we'll look for another bedsit.'

I agreed. 'Definitely,' I said.

It took me ages to get to sleep. I tossed and turned and every so often I would hear the front door opening and closing. There would be loud voices, more doors slamming and then quiet. Then it would start over again. Eventually I dropped off to sleep.

I was awoken by a loud knocking on the front door. A blue light was revolving around the bedsit. Startled, I threw the bed covers back and went over to the

12

window and peeped through the opening in the curtains. 'Oh my God, Katie, it's the police,' I said.

No one is opening the front door of the building and I wonder what to do.

'Do you think we should go down and open it?' I ask Katie.

'Don't be daft,' she says, 'We'd better stay out of it. It's got nothing to do with us.'

I open the curtains a little further. Mrs Lowe is coming up the path. She's wearing a dressing gown, a nightcap on her head and slippers on her feet. She's carrying a torch. I can hear shouting and loud voices from outside but not what is being said. Slowly I open the window.

'This is a respectable house, officer,' Mrs Lowe is saying. She unlocks the front door and around four policemen rush inside. There is a lot of shouting and soon someone is being taken out of the house and down the path. He's protesting his innocence.

'I wasn't there, officer, I've been in me bed all night,' he is pleading.

Another lad is brought out. He's not so compliant. He's fighting and tussling with two police officers.

'Get off me ya fucking polis bastards,' he's shouting in his Scottish accent.

'Now then, Billy, you'll only make it worse for yourself,' a policeman says as he drags him along. They take him out and put him in the police car. The doors are slammed shut and the car speeds away.

Katie joins me at the window. 'No wonder Tania warned us to keep our door locked, there's thieves living downstairs,' she says.

'And Mrs Lowe says she doesn't want any riffraff in the house. They're already here!' I reply.

We watch as Mrs Lowe makes her way back down the path. She straightens her night cap.

'She looks funny, doesn't she? She reminds me of Wee Willie Winkie,' I say.

Just then she turns around and looks up at the window.

'Oooh, I think she's heard you,' Katie laughs. 'Quick, don't let her see us looking, she might think we've got something to do with it.' We get back into our beds.

'I won't be able to get back to sleep now,' Katie says.

'Me neither. I have to give that woman her cigarettes an' all,' I reply.

'Yeah, you'd better,' Katie laughs, 'she might come here looking for you.'

'This is a mad house. What have we got ourselves into?' We both start giggling.

'I'm not staying in this house for long,' I say.

THE POLICEMEN CALL

The next morning Katie accompanies me as I knock on the door of number five. It is opened by a woman wearing a bri-nylon nightdress. She looks middle aged, certainly not a teenager. She's wearing rollers in her hair under a chiffon scarf. Pale blue button eyes look at me inquisitively.

'Can I help you?' she asks as she elegantly puffs on a cigarette.

'I've brought the cigarettes the woman asked me to get from the shop,' I say as I hand her the packet and the change in coins.

'She won't remember a thing about it,' comes the reply.

'Who is it Jo?' a voice calls out. The woman opens the door wider. 'Come in,' she says.

She turns and walks back into the room. Katie hesitates but I push her inside. I'm not going in there on my own, I think.

The room is much larger than our bedsit. The woman I saw the night before is sitting up in a king size bed. She's wearing blue pyjamas and holding a cigarette in her hand. There's a bedside locker next to the bed with a half filled cup of tea on top.

'Oh, hello,' she says. 'I remember you from the stairs. So, I wasn't dreaming after all! Come and sit on me bed and bring your friend with you.'

'Faye, do behave yourself,' the woman scolds.

Faye grins. 'Only kidding, you can sit here,' she says, pointing to an ottoman that's beside the bed. Katie and I sit down.

'I'm Faye,' she tells us, 'and this is Josie. I call her Jo for short. Are you and her one of us?'

I am thinking she's asking if we have moved in.

'Yes,' I say.

'Ooh, that's interesting,' she replies.

She rubs her forehead.

'Ooh, I've got a splitting headache. Fetch us a couple of aspirin, will you, Jo? I could do with a hair of the dog an' all,' she says.

'It's too early for that,' Jo replies. 'Haven't you had enough after last night? And besides, I haven't forgotten that I'm not speaking to you after what you said to my gentleman friend.'

'Don't remember much about it, Jo, honestly,' she says, looking at me and winking behind Jo's back.

Jo turns and gives her a black look. I get the feeling that she's heard it all before.

'Make our guests a cup of char, Jo,' Faye says. She obviously wants us to stay.

'So, you're Anne and you come from the North East,' she says. I'm surprised that she remembers me telling her. She looks at Katie.

'Is this your girlfriend?' she asks. 'What's her name?' I don't cotton on to what she means by 'girlfriend'.

'This is Katie,' I say. 'I met her at a wedding.' She turns to Katie.

'You got a good-looking one there,' she says. 'Lucky you!' Katie blushes.

'We're just good friends,' she stammers.

Faye grins. 'Like me and Jo, eh?' she says as she blows circles of cigarette smoke from her lips. I am puzzled.

Jo brings me and Katie a cup of tea. Now she is fussing around wiping the bedside locker where Faye has spilled tea and cigarette ash.

There is a gentle knock on the door.

'Who is it?' Faye shouts.

'It's me, Liam, bearing gifts,' a high-pitched voice shouts. Jo opens the door. A skinny fair-haired young man wearing silk pyjamas enters the room. He places a packet of cigarettes on the bedside locker. 'Payback time,' he says. He goes over to the armchair and smoothes over the seat before sitting down. He lights a cigarette with long slender fingers then crosses his legs. A slipper is left dangling from his foot.

So, this is the Liam who has a bedsit on the top floor, I think. The one who plays his records all the time and who Tania says is suicidal.

He sees Katie and I. 'Friends of yours, Faye?' he asks. She nods.

'This is Anne and Katie,' Faye says. 'They arrived yesterday from the North East. They've come here looking for jobs. They've got Lackey's bedsit.'

'Welcome to the Den of Iniquity,' he says. 'You don't know what you're letting yourselves in for!'

I wonder why everyone calls it that, but then, after last night, I suppose I shouldn't be surprised.

'You've got some nice records,' Katie says, making an effort to be friendly. 'I heard you playing *Paint it Black* by the *Rolling Stones*. I like that one.'

Oh, trust Katie to put her foot in it, I think. He was probably playing that because he was feeling low.

'You can borrow it, but don't scratch it,' he replies.

'Ah, thanks,' Katie says. 'We can do a swap. Do you like Billy Fury? Anne does, her favourite record is *Halfway to Paradise*.'

I wish Katie would shut up.

'Not my scene,' he says.

'I like the Beatles,' I say.

'Ooh, I don't like insects,' Liam says. Katie and I start giggling.

He turns his attention to Faye.

'What was all that commotion about last night, then? Who were they looking for this time?' he says.

'I was out for the count, but Jo heard it all,' Faye replies.

'They reckon Scots Billy and Dougie turned over a warehouse,' Jo says.

'Did they?' Liam asks.

'What do you think?' Faye says, as she blows more circles of smoke in the air.

'The cops never found anything when they searched their rooms. They were fuming, thought they'd caught them red handed. Couldn't find any evidence, but they've charged Scots Billy with resisting arrest as he clouted one of the policemen. He's up in court this morning,' Jo tells us.

'What about Dougie?' he asks.

'He's been released. He was up here earlier on,' Jo replies.

'Who's Scots Billy?' Katie asks.

'He's got a bedsit on the ground floor,' Jo says.

'And he's got a right temper on him,' Liam adds.

Jo brings Liam a cup of tea. 'Do you want a slice of toast?' she asks.

'No thanks, I'm on a diet,' Liam says. 'When Robbie gets out I want to be slim and gorgeous.'

I wonder why he is on a diet and think to myself that he could do with a good meal as there is nothing on him.

'Have you heard from him?' Faye asks.

'Yes, I got a letter from him,' he says. Out of the top pocket of his pyjamas he produces the folded letter and kisses it.

'What does he say?' Faye asks.

'Ooh, I couldn't tell you that, Faye. He's talking about all the things he's going to do to me when he gets out.'

Faye frowns. 'I wouldn't have thought a letter like that would have got past the prison guards? I'd have thought it'd be censored,' she says.

'It should have been. I bet it turned them on,' Liam giggles.

There's a loud knock on the door.

'Bloody 'ell, who's that?' Faye exclaims. 'It sounds like the cops.' She lowers her voice and adds, 'Don't open it yet, Jo.'

'Just you two stay there and don't move,' she warns Katie and me.

'Why? We haven't done anything,' Katie says.

Faye puts a finger to her lips. 'Shush,' she whispers. Liam stubs out his cigarette, gets up and goes over to the bed. He crawls over Faye and gets into bed next to her. He lies on his side.

'I'm asleep, if anyone asks,' he says and pulls the cover over his head. I am wondering what on earth is going on. There is another loud knock on the door. Faye looks around and when satisfied she says, 'You'd better let them in, Jo.'

'I do apologise,' Jo says, as she opens the door. 'I was in a state of undress.' She still is, I think. She's wearing her nightdress.

'Come in, officer,' Faye shouts from the bed. 'How are you? Come and sit down. Jo will make you a cuppa.'

Two police officers come into the room. One is wearing his police helmet. It is obvious that both Faye and Jo are on friendly terms with these two.

The older officer sits on the side of her bed. The other one sits in the armchair.

'Want a ciggie?' Faye asks and stretches out a packet towards him.

'Don't mind if I do,' he replies. Jo is at his shoulder with a cigarette lighter. He lights the cigarette, takes a deep breath, inhales the smoke deep into his lungs then slowly exhales.

'Ah, that's better, we're not allowed to smoke on duty,' he tells us.

'You don't smoke, do you, Ginger?' Faye says to the other officer. He shakes his head and takes off his helmet to reveal a mop of bright ginger hair.

'Now then, Faye,' the senior officer says. 'Do you know anything about this warehouse break in? We believe Scots Billy and Dougie were involved.'

'Not heard a thing officer, honestly,' Faye says. 'Is that what the raid was all about last night?'

'Yes, and we know them buggers were involved. It's just proving it, that's all,' the officer replies.

'We have two new tenants,' Faye tells him. 'Anne and Katie, they moved in yesterday'.

The policeman looks us up and down. 'Can't say I've seen either of them before,' he says.

'They just came here from the North East,' Faye replies.

'You're not working girls are you?' he asks.

I am going to be looking for a job soon so I say, 'Not yet, but I hope to be in the next couple of days.'

The ginger cop stares at me. He looks shocked.

The senior officer tuts. 'My advice to you young ladies is to get back home. This isn't the place for you,' he tells us.

There is a titter from under the blankets. Liam stirs. 'Who the bloody hell is that?' the senior officer says as he jumps off the bed. Liam pops his head up from under the covers. He rubs his eyes. 'Where am I?' he asks.

'You must have had a skinful last night,' the officer says, 'if you ended up in bed with Faye.'

Faye laughs.

'Hope you are not thinking of doing anything silly now,' the officer says to Liam. 'He's not worth it. He's trouble is that one.'

They must be referring to Liam's boyfriend, Robbie, I think.

'He's always in and out of the nick an' all,' Faye says.

'And he's married,' Jo chips in.

'Where did you meet him?' the ginger officer asks.

'Strangeways,' Liam replies.

I'm sure Faye told me that was a prison, I think to myself.

'Would you like a ginger biscuit, officer?' Jo asks.

'Yes, specially got 'em for you,' Faye says to Ginger. He grins and blushes.

'How is the old man?' the senior officer enquires.

'He's in hospital,' Faye says. 'The malaria flared up again. He was sweating buckets and having nightmares and crying out. He thought he was back in the camps.'

'He didn't want to go to the hospital,' Jo says, 'but Mrs Lowe insisted. They had to sedate him. He thought they were taking him to the gas chamber.'

'How awful, hasn't he any family?' the officer asks.

'No, they've all gone. He's Eastern European. He doesn't speak English. But Mrs Lowe understands him,' Faye replies.

The older officer finishes his tea and wipes his mouth with the back of his hand.

'Well, must be going, Faye, there's lots of criminals to catch. Thanks for the cuppa,' he says. 'If you do hear anything give us a bell, will you?'

Faye nods. 'Certainly will, officer,' she says. 'We don't want any riffraff in this house.'

The ginger officer gets up from the chair. He hands his cup to Jo. 'Thanks for the cuppa and the bics,' he says, smiling at Katie and I.

'You two lasses stay out of trouble,' the senior officer says.

I am quite affronted. I have no intention of getting into trouble. The last time I'd had anything to do with the police was when I ran away from Nazareth House. I wonder if I have a criminal record.

Jo sees the policemen out of the door.

'Put the latch on the door, Jo,' Faye says. She turns to Katie and me.

'You did a grand job,' she tells us. 'We kept the officer talking and Ginger couldn't take his eyes of you in your mini skirt. He couldn't string two words together. Mind you, I don't blame him.'

She's grinning. 'Right then, stand up both of you,' she says.

Why is she ordering us to do that? I'm puzzled. 'Just stand up,' she says. Katie and I get up off the ottoman.

'Go on Jo, open it,' she says. Jo comes over to where we have been sitting. She opens the lid of the Ottoman. Inside, there are dresses, shoes, jewellery and God knows what else.

'They're them stolen goods them cops have been looking for,' Faye says. 'Dougie sneaked them up here last night.' Katie's jaw drops.

'Eee, we might have got arrested,' she says.

I'm too shocked for words.

BLOOD DONOR

Katie and I decided to walk into Manchester city centre as we couldn't afford to get the bus. It was quite a long walk but we were eager to find out what this great city had to offer. We had heard lots about it. We strolled along Deansgate. I felt dwarfed by the tall buildings that were on either side. Along the way we saw posters of George Best. I'd heard about this George Best he was the reason that I was a football fan.' I'd love to meet him, I said. I'm going to get his autograph if we do. Do you think that we will bump into him?' I asked Katie. 'If we do I'm going to ask him for a date.' She said.

'You'll have to dye your hair Katie I've heard that he likes girls with blonde hair.

'I would for him,' she said.

I'd seen photographs of the footballer in Magazines. He was either posing with a blonde girl on his arm or sitting in some fast expensive car.

There were coloured pictures of him either in the red Manchester United kit or there were black and white photos of him wearing the latest sixties fashion and with a hairstyle similar to the Beatles.

'Hasn't he got gorgeous eyes,' I said. Katie agreed.' He should be a film star not a footballer she said.

We ambled along just soaking up the sounds and the smells of this great city. Hoping to somehow bump into Georgie Best.

We ended up in Piccadilly Gardens where we sat on a bench to rest our sore feet. The imposing statue of

Queen Victoria looked down on us as we observed the people passing by. There were crowds of people making their way to and from the nearby bus station. Everything seemed bigger and busier than our home town and so exciting. We had a wander along the high street, stopping every so often to gaze in a shop window to admire the latest sixties fashions. It was all we could do, as we had no money to spend. It was fun going up and down the escalator in the John Lewis store although a little scary. I'd never been on one before.

On the pavement outside we came across a large notice board. It was placed outside the door of one of the buildings. It was an advertisement for blood donors. 'Your blood can save a life,' it read.

'I'm going to go in and give some blood,' I said.

'What? You must be mad,' Katie replied.

But I wasn't doing it for some gallant reason.

The notice board also read, 'Free tea and biscuits available afterwards.' I was hungry and also I was curious. 'I'll come in with you,' Katie said, 'but I'm not giving them any of my blood.'

I wasn't too scared of needles. I'd been immunised against tuberculosis. At school I remember waiting in a queue to have my injection. Most of the girls were apprehensive, some were terrified and one even fainted. I think the reason I'd been stoic is that one of the girls had told me about the horrors of the disease.

'Me grandad had it,' she'd said. 'Your lungs turn green and they rot away.' I'd been scared and I didn't want that happening to me. Having the injection seemed such a small price to pay.

Katie and I walked up some steps and made our way into the building. The woman at the reception desk wanted my details and asked about my medical history. I gave my name and date of birth. 'Have you had any of these?' she asked as she went through a list of diseases.

'I've had ringworm,' I told her. 'When I was eight years old.' I didn't tell her that the nuns had shaved my head. She might have thought that I'd had a particularly virulent form of the fungus infection.

'What about you?' she asked Katie. 'Would you like to donate blood? It's for a good cause.'

'Ooh no,' Katie said. 'I'm terrified of needles.' The woman went over to see the nurse. 'I'll tell her I've got some kind of illness,' Katie whispered, 'if she asks me again.'

Before long I was lying on a bed with a needle in my arm. 'How much blood will I be giving?' I asked the nurse.

'Just one pint,' she said. *One pint!* I was alarmed. It was just as well I was lying down. I started to think maybe this wasn't such a good idea. 'Your body will soon make it up,' she said reassuringly.

'You will know when to stop?' I asked. 'You won't take too much?'

She laughed. 'Of course not,' she said. Katie was sat near me screwing her face up as she watched my blood dripping into the plastic container.

'Just think of a pint of milk,' the nurse said. 'That's the equivalent of what you're giving.'

'Yes, but I'll get a blood donor card then I can brag that I've given blood.'

'Is that all?' Katie said. 'You deserve a medal.' I think she was impressed.

There were other people giving blood. 'Have you done this before?' I asked a middle-aged man who was lying on a bed nearby. 'Yes, over twenty times,' he said proudly.

'He's just bragging,' Katie said in a quiet voice. 'He'd be dead if he'd given that much.'

I had to lie down for a short time afterwards. Then, Katie and I were given tea and biscuits. Although she wasn't entitled, I told the nurse that she had offered me moral support.

'You will get a blood donor card, it will come in the post,' the nurse said.

'How do you feel after losing all that blood?' Katie asked when we got outside.

'I feel a lot lighter,' I replied.

'Really?' she asked.

'Yes, but if I get tired on the long walk back to the bedsit, you'll have to give me a piggy back,' I said.

'Do you think we should get the bus?' Katie said, looking concerned. 'I could tell the conductor that you've feeling faint.'

'Nah, I'm only kidding. I'm fine,' I said.

A few weeks later I was the proud owner of a blood donor card. It informed me that my blood group was B rhesus positive, one of the rarer types. I felt quite pleased with myself for donating my blood and hoped it had gone to some worthy person.

SOCIAL SECURITY

'We'll have to get money from the social,' Katie said, 'or we won't be able to pay next week's rent.'

'And we have no coins to put in the gas meter,' I added.

We were sitting on our beds figuring out what we would need to say at the social security office. We had put it off for as long as we could in the hope that we'd both find jobs, but reality had set in.

'We'll probably have to work a week's notice before we get paid,' Katie said, 'and if we get work in a factory we'll have to buy our own overalls.'

We had been in Manchester for a week and were down to our last few pence. Tania had helped us out by giving us a packet of tealeaves and custard cream biscuits, and Jo kept us going with bacon butties and many cups of tea. In return we would run errands for them. Usually it was to get cigarettes from the shop. Luckily neither Katie nor I smoked. Liam helped by giving us his loose change for the gas meter. In between I lived on a bottle of milk and a Mars bar.

'Get yourselves down to the social,' Faye said one day while we were enjoying a plate of chip butties that Jo had made for us. 'Tell em you're pregnant. Say you're havin' twins or triplets. That'll get you summit. Say yer fella's done a moonlight flit, and you can't find him.'

Eventually we went along and joined the long queue at the social security office. We gave our names at reception, and then we had to sit in the waiting area until our names were called. Katie had decided that she would try to claim the rent money for the bedsit and she had taken the rent book with her.

I would claim for myself. I was nervous as I hadn't done this before. I bombarded Katie with questions.

'What do I say?' I asked her.

'Tell them that you've been thrown out of your home and have come to Manchester looking for work. And that you are skint and have nothing to live on.'

'Won't they ask why I could not find a job nearer to home?'

'Just tell them you had come to Manchester to live near relatives.'

'Won't they ask why I couldn't live with them?'

'You can't,' Katie replied. 'There is no room in their house.'

'What if they asked me for their address?'

'They won't.'

'What if they do?'

'Make one up.'

'What if they find out I'm telling fibs?'

'Tell them you accidentally gave them the wrong address.'

'I hope they don't ask me for my home address,' I said. 'I haven't got one and I don't want to tell them I was in Nazzie House either.'

We were surrounded by crying babies, bored kids and tired mothers. One mother had four bairns and I felt sorry for her. She had bruises on her face and looked worn out.

'I'm gonna belt you if you don't get down,' she screamed at one of the kids who was jumping up and down on the seat. One toddler was whimpering and tugging at her sleeve, obviously wanting attention. She was giving her baby a bottle and trying to keep an eye on her older children. I had a small mirror in my bag so I took it out and let the toddler see his face. He was pulling out his tongue but at least it kept him occupied while his poor mother got on with feeding her baby. We waited for hours before my name was called. I was taken into a booth to be interviewed by a matronly woman wearing a twin set and a pearl necklace. 'Pearls are unlucky,' my mother had said, but I thought that strange as she often wore them herself. Maybe that's why she didn't have much luck.

'What's your address?' the woman asked in a rather stern voice. It suddenly occurred to me that I had forgotten the number of the house where we were staying. I racked my brains trying to think of it while she impatiently tapped her pen on the table. Maybe if I told her its tenants call it the Den of Iniquity she might know it. No, maybe not. I tried to explain. 'It's a big house in Bury Old Road,' I said. 'It's a three figure number.'

I don't think she believed me.

Exasperated, she sighed.

'We will need proof that you are living there,' she said.

'What was your last place of employment?' she asked. I had worked for a short time as a waitress in Sparks' Café in Stockton on Tees so I mentioned that.

'Why did you leave your local area?' she asked.

I wanted to say, 'To see the bright lights of Manchester, have some fun. If you'd been cooped up in an orphanage run by nuns for thirteen years you would too.' But that's not a good answer, I thought.

I just shrugged my shoulders and let her think I had something to hide.

'You will have to sign on at the labour exchange. You will also have to wait six weeks to get paid as you left your previous position voluntary.' I still had to sign my name.

'That was a waste of time,' I said to Katie, who'd had no luck either.

'We have to sign on the dole,' she said, 'or we won't get a penny from them.'

'I'm fed up,' I said. 'I'm going to look for a job today.'

At the labour exchange there was a job advertised for a barmaid with an immediate start. I had never worked in a pub before. The thought of pulling pints and then adding the sums up didn't appeal to me but still I decided to give it a go.

We wrote down a few details of other jobs. There was a job advertised for a filing clerk at a mail order firm and for a packer in a biscuit factory in Crumpsall. There was even one for a go-go dancer. 'Do you think I should apply?' Katie laughed.

'Go on, I dare you,' I said. 'You can borrow my knee length boots.'

THE INTERVIEW

My interview was at ten o'clock in the morning. It seemed alien walking into a pub, never mind working in one. But I needed to earn the money so that we could pay the rent and eventually move to a decent bedsit. I had to pluck up the courage to go in. I very nearly backed out. I pressed on the doorbell. I waited, no one came. I pressed it again. I was about to walk away when I heard a key turning in the lock. The door was swung open. A man with dark shoulder length hair appeared. He looked as if he was in his thirties. He was heavily tanned and he wore a frilly shirt open to the waist revealing a hairy chest. 'Have you come to see me?' he asked. 'I can't keep the women from the door,' he grinned.

He was good-looking but something about him told me he thought that he was God's gift to women and the weeks ahead would prove me right.

'I've come about the barmaid's job,' I said.

'Come in,' he said. We sat down at a table in the lounge. He sat opposite me.

'Right then, have you any experience?' he asked.

'None at all.'

'Oh, so you're a virgin?'

I blushed.

'I've never worked as a barmaid before,' I said.

'Oh, we'll soon break you in,' he grinned. 'How old are you?'

'Eighteen.'

'Well, you're old enough,' he said.

I didn't like his interview-style. It made me uneasy. There was a middle-aged woman wiping the tables down. She looked at us warily.

'Your duties will be to take orders, serve drinks and snacks and wash glasses,' he said. 'And if you want to earn extra tips,' he added, lowering his voice and winking, 'keep the landlord happy. Come on, I'll show you round.' We passed through the bar.

'I'll teach you how to pull pints when you start,' he said. I followed him up the stairs to his living quarters. We went through the living room and passed a bedroom. The door was open and I could see that the bed was unmade, as if someone had simply crawled out of it. I'm not going in there, I thought. We passed another room and the door was also open. It was a nursery, newly decorated. He quickly closed the door. I wondered what I was doing upstairs when I would be working downstairs. The cleaning woman was making her presence felt. She stomped up the stairs.

'Don't forget, you need to change the taps, Maurice,' she shouted.

'I haven't forgotten, *thank you!*' he answered irritably.

'When will you be bringing your wife and the baby home from the hospital?' she asked. I got the feeling she emphasised 'wife and baby' for my benefit.

'She's in for a few days yet,' he said.

'It's not like in my day. You were up and about as soon as you had it.'

He seemed annoyed. I was quite glad of the interruption.

He went down the stairs. I followed him. She was keeping a watchful eye on us. She obviously thought he was up to something.

'Take no notice of her,' he said quietly. 'She's just a nosy old bat. Right then, do you want the job?' He didn't wait for an answer. 'It will be five pounds to do the evening shift, and three quid if you do the daytime.' That seemed a fortune to me and I thought I might be able to pave the way for Katie too. I should have said no, but Katie and I were desperate. I had no option but to accept the job.

'Can you start tomorrow?' he asked.

'Yes,' I said. Now there was no going back.

'Be here for ten o'clock,' he said. He escorted me to the door. The cleaning woman had come down the stairs, and although pretending to polish the bar she was keeping a beady eye on us. She may not have known it, but I was glad that she was there.

He came outside in the pretence of doing something to the door all the while gawping at me as I made my way down the road. I wished I had worn my maxi skirt. I felt quite undressed in my mini skirt and knee length white go-go boots.

BARMAID

On Saturday I arrived at ten o'clock to start work in the pub. The cleaning woman was there and she looked at me as if to say, 'I'm keeping an eye on you.' She needn't have worried as I was not in the least bit interested in Maurice.

There was a young man behind the bar. He smiled at me.

'Are you the new girl?' he asked. 'We were expecting you.' I went behind the bar.

'I've never done this before,' I said. 'I'm quite nervous.'

'Don't worry. You'll soon get the hang of it. I'll help you out if you get stuck.'

'I haven't a clue about measures of whisky and gin,' I said.

'How do I pull a pint?' I asked him.

'You really are new to this,' he said.

'Yes, I mean it when I say I've never done this before.'

Maurice came into the bar.

'Hello,' he said. 'You made it, then? I'll let you have a practise before the customers come in. Pour me a pint.'

'I don't know how to,' I said. 'I've never done it before.'

He came up behind me and stood far too close for comfort. He reached up and got a pint glass down. When I tried to pull pints they either came out too frothy, or I overfilled the glass, or I didn't fill them up enough. I'll never be able to do this, I thought.

The morning was a disaster. I got all flummoxed and Paul had to take over my orders but was really patient with me. The pub was filling up. I got all hot and bothered when I got a large order. I struggled to add up the bill. I would repeatedly ask Paul to check it and it was frequently wrong. Maths was never my strongest subject at school. Although he himself was busy serving other customers he was always courteous to me. He was a real gentleman. It was also difficult to hear above the noise. Many a time I had to ask a customer to repeat their order. If it wasn't for Paul I think that I would have given up and walked out there and then. In a quieter moment, Paul told me that he and his girlfriend were saving up to get married. He worked in a factory during the day but in the evenings and at the weekends he worked as a barman.

'You must never see your girlfriend,' I said.

'Oh, she comes and sits at the bar sometimes,' he replied.

On the other hand, God's Gift to Women was always hovering around, making me nervous. He would try to get me to stay back after closing time on the pretence of teaching me more about the trade. But, I was wary of him.

'Where are you going after work?' he would ask. 'Why don't you stay back? I'll show you how to pull the pints properly.'

I watched the way he made a beeline for the women. He would be chatting them up and making lewd suggestions. I thought that the way he treated women was very disrespectful. I felt sorry for his wife in more ways than one. Apparently, she'd had problems after giving birth by caesarean to a baby girl. This meant a longer stay in hospital. Maurice made the most of this opportunity and I would frequently see women going up to his living quarters. However, it didn't stop him harassing me.

THE CLUB

It was Friday evening. Katie and I were watching television on an old black and white set. We had been in Manchester a couple of weeks and I had earned my first week's wages. Katie had also got a job at Marshall Ward, the mail order firm. There was a knock on the door. It was Tania. She was wearing a white fake fur coat. 'Do you fancy having a night out?' she said. Liam was working behind a bar in a club downtown and she was going to pop in to see him.

We hadn't intended on going out. Our intention was to get some money together so that we could afford a decent bedsit. Besides, we'd hardly brought any clothes with us.

'I've got nothing to wear,' Katie said.

'I'll lend you summit,' Tania said. She went into her own room and came back carrying a couple of dresses.

Tania was quite petite so her dresses were too small for me but Katie was able to borrow one that fitted her.

I had a brown suede mini skirt and a yellow skinny rib polo neck jumper. They were in fashion, but my knee length white boots were my favourite item of clothing. I wore them everywhere.

Katie and I took it in turns to stand in front of the mirror to apply eyeliner and lashings of black mascara. We applied so many coats of mascara that by the time we had finished it looked as if we were wearing false ones. 'I look like Twiggy,' she said, but it was all the fashion then.

On Cheetham Hill Road we hailed a black taxi to take us downtown.

We arrived at the club and we had to pay to get in. We went downstairs into a smoky, dimly lit room. I could barely see. Katie and I followed Tania to the bar where Liam was serving.

'Who let you riffraff in,' he grinned, as he handed Tania a gin and tonic.

'We've escaped from the Den of Iniquity,' she said.

'What do you want to drink?' he asked Katie and me.

Although I worked in a pub I had only ever had a sip of alcohol. Katie wanted a beer and she asked for half a bitter. 'I'll have the same,' I said, not wanting to be left out.

'These are on the house,' Liam whispered.

There was a lad stood at the bar. Tania knew him. 'That's Dean, Liam's friend,' she said. He was waiting for Liam to finish work. Tania introduced Katie and me and she invited Dean to come and join us.

'Let's find a seat,' she said.

She looked around. We three followed her to a table near a little stage. It was a squeeze but we managed to sit down and place our drinks on the beer mats on the table. There was an air of expectancy in the room and men were hogging the front of the stage. I took a sip of beer and its fiery taste burnt my throat and made me shiver. When I was in Nazareth House we girls often wondered what beer would taste like. 'It's horrible,' Pam Cahill had told us but it hadn't stopped her getting completely kaylied one afternoon.

We had been working in the upstairs nursery and it was her half day off. A friend from school, one of the 'outside girls' as we called them, had taken her to the pub for the first time. Mari, Jeannie and I had done our best to hide her from the nuns. Unfortunately, important visitors were being shown round that day. I will never forget Sister Wulstan's face on finding Pam in the laundry room where we'd tried to hide her. She couldn't stand up and she'd been as sick as a dog.

'You brazen hussy,' she had called her.

What would Sister Wulstan think of me now? I took another sip of beer. Cheers, Sister Wulstan! Here's to another brazen hussy, I thought.

Tania interrupted my musings.

'Oh, you got to see this drag act,' she said, 'he's dead funny.'

A man jumped up on the stage. He was dressed in a glitzy shirt and wearing makeup. He was the warm-up for the forthcoming act. He exchanged banter with the men in the audience and even Dean got involved. The compere then introduced somebody called Lola.

'That's a man,' Tania whispered. 'Wait until you see him, he's brilliant.'

Lola came on stage impersonating Marlene Dietrich. He wore a top hat, white jacket, fishnet stockings, and high heels and was carrying a cane. He got a rowdy reception from the audience. He placed one leg on a chair. 'Falling in love again,' he sang in a slow sensuous manner. When he'd finished his act, he was greeted with rapturous applause, whistling and cat callings galore.

I'd seen pantomime dames when we had been taken to the Globe in Stockton on Tees. They were overdressed and heavily made up but this was a feminine guy. I'd never seen anything like it. I was mesmerised.

Since coming to live in Manchester, I'd learn that 'queer' had a different meaning to the one in the English dictionary. I was totally ignorant and had no idea that two men or indeed two women could have a sexual relationship. It was not something the nuns talked about. Sex was a taboo subject in Nazareth House. Even when a girl started her period we were not taught anything about the facts of life. She would be given a book about Mary the Virgin Mother. There was no mention of sexual intercourse. As a result many girls left Nazareth house with no idea how babies were conceived. We had to find out for ourselves.

I looked around the room and watched the guys interact with each other. Some stayed on the sidelines observing the action on the dance floor. One good-looking lad bounced into the room surrounded by friends. He attracted a lot of attention. The reaction was much the same as it would have been with a pretty girl. He caused quite a stir. Dean especially took a liking to him. 'He's hooked,' Tania said.

When Lola left the stage, Tania said that she had to see to business.

Katie and I warned her to be careful. She laughed. 'You sound like me mother,' she said.

But we had good reason to be concerned. Earlier in the year two girls had hitch-hiked a lift. They were missing for months before they were eventually found. They had been murdered. It had been all over the news.

Katie and I watched as she made her way out of the room. We had come to like Tania and we didn't want anything nasty happening to her.

Tania had told us that she was working as a prostitute. I was surprised, and even more so at how blasé she was about it.

'Why does she take the risk?' Katie asked. It's not as if she has kids to keep.

'Don't you get scared?' I asked her. 'Nah, I don't do it in their car. I've got a friend in Moss Side. She lets me use her room. I give her a couple of bob.'

'What if you end up with someone who's freaky?' Katie asked.

'If anyone tries any funny business, I know how to handle them,' she said.

'We wouldn't do that for all the tea in China,' Katie and I agreed.

'I earn more dough in one night as you two get in a week,' she'd said. 'And besides, I enjoy it.'

There was no arguing with that.

She certainly earned the money and could afford the latest fashionable clothes from the George Best Boutique. She knew all the answers, or thought she did, but I didn't envy her at all.

'Let's dance?' Dean said as he grabbed me by the arm. 'I daren't,' I said. I'd no confidence to get up and dance but boosted by the alcohol I soon changed my mind. I dragged Katie up and before long we were doing our own version of the twist. It was the only dance that I knew. Dean was a good dancer. Soon we were, or rather he was, the centre of attention. If his aim was to get the good-looking guy interested he certainly had his attention now.

We sat down. I was feeling tipsy. When Katie and I left the club, Dean and the good-looking guy were making eyes at each other.

FAYE AND JO

Faye and Jo's bedsit was where we tenants would congregate. They loved having company and Jo would always be on hand with bacon or chip butties, or just a biscuit and a cup of char, as Faye called it. 'I should open a cafe,' Jo said. 'I would make a fortune.'

Faye was popular. Jo was the long suffering 'wife'. If anyone was down on their luck they could always count on Faye to lend them a couple of bob, much to Jo's annoyance as sometimes it would never be repaid.

Katie, myself, and Tania were frequent visitors to their bedsit. We all lived on the same floor and would often see each other when we were coming up or down the stairs.

At the weekends Faye would be out on the town while Jo met her 'gentlemen friends', as she called them. They were her regulars. Faye's favourite tipple was whisky and we would often pass her on the stairs the worse for wear. The amount that she would drink I was surprised that she could stand. She would not touch a drop of alcohol for weeks and then she would go on a binge.

She was as cheerful when she was drunk as when she was sober, but often tried to kiss me.

'Behave yourself, Faye,' I would scold her. 'Whatever would Jo say?' She would grin and take it all with good humour. 'No harm in trying,' she would say.

We enjoyed the banter between them. It was akin to Morecambe and Wise.

Faye was impulsive, loud and generous. Jo was more reticent, quiet and thoughtful.

'How did you and Jo meet?' Katie asked her. We were sat in their bedsit having a cup of tea.

'She asked me out,' Faye said. 'She couldn't resist me cos I'm tall, dark and handsome.'

'I asked you out?' Jo retorted. 'You begged me for a date. You even got down on one knee.'

'I was blind drunk at the time,' Faye winked at us.

'If you were drunk,' Jo said, 'then I was blind. Blind to what I was letting myself in for.' Faye grinned.

'She was married, you know. Left her fella for me,' Faye said proudly. 'She never knew what she was missing 'til she got with me.'

Jo rolled her eyes and said, 'She thinks she's god's gift to woman.' Faye laughed.

'Maurice thinks he is,' I said

'Yes, I've heard all about him,' Jo said. 'He's a womaniser. He's been married before. She's his second wife.'

'The barman said that he's got another girl up the stick,' I said. 'He's been messing about with other women while his wife was pregnant. She caught him in bed with the barmaid, Paul told me. That's the one I've replaced. She's given him a warning. No wonder that cleaning woman was keeping an eye on me.

'If he doesn't stop pestering me, I'm looking for another job.'

Faye frowned. 'Think I'll have to have a word with this Maurice,' she said.

'Don't you dare,' Jo said. 'Anne will lose her job.'

'His wife's coming home with the baby soon,' I said. 'I'm sure she'll keep an eye on him.'

'If he gets too fresh,' Faye said, 'kick him where it hurts, in the balls.'

ROBBIE

Arriving at the house I notice a man walking up our pathway. He sees me heading in the same direction and stops to let me pass. He has short cropped hair which is unusual as most guys wear their hair quite long. It is the fashion. He is good-looking in a rough kind of way. I open the front door. He passes me without saying a word and heads for the stairs. Maybe he's a new tenant, I think. I follow him up the stairs. I stop at the second floor but he goes on up the stairs. I wonder if he's heading for Liam's room. I go into my bedsit. Katie is not back yet. I sit on my bed. I am looking forward to spending a lazy afternoon reading some magazines that Tania has given me; *The New Musical Express*, *The Jackie* and *Vogue*, which features the model Jean Shrimpton on the cover. There is a knock on the door. Thinking it is Katie I shout, 'Have you forgotten your key?' I open the door. It's the man I saw on the path.

'Have you seen Liam?' he asks.

'I haven't,' I say. 'I've not seen him today. I've been out.' He swears under his breath.

'Tell him I've been here and I'm not hanging around like a wanker. I'm going home and I'm not fucking coming back,' he says angrily. He storms off down the stairs, opens the front door and slams it behind him. That's one angry fellow, I think.

Katie comes back from work and she is bubbling. 'The jobs dead easy but boring,' she says. 'I'm just filing cards at the moment. It's a great atmosphere. We

47

have a good laugh. The line manager is gorgeous but married. All the girls fancy him. There's talk that he's having it off with a girl from the typing.

'One of the girls kept being sick in the loo. She's pregnant but she's not married and hasn't told her parents. She says her dad will kill her if he finds out. She asked me not to say anything. She's frightened she'll lose her job.

'What about the boyfriend?' I ask.

'*He's* chased *her* but he's married and he's seeing someone else. Men are shit,' she says.

CHANGING JOBS

I was getting better at serving behind the bar. If it was busy I'd still get flummoxed, but Paul would help me out. There were the regulars who hung around the bar. I got lots of tips, especially when the pub was busy. There were many office workers who came in their lunch hour or after work. They wouldn't bother waiting for their change, especially if it was a small amount. 'Keep the change,' they'd say, or, 'have one yourself'. I saved my tips and kept them in a glass jar.

There were many women who came to see Maurice. I felt sorry for his wife.

One woman was a regular. She'd sit on a stool at the bar trying to catch his attention. She couldn't take her eyes of him.

'She's probably an old flame,' Paul said, 'but he's lost interest.'

'Why do they still hang around when they know he's married?'

'He obviously encourages them,' Paul said, 'but he just uses them.'

At closing time we would see the customers off then we had to stay behind and wash the glasses and clear up.

Maurice would be hovering around. He would creep up behind me and put his hands on my shoulders.

'Bet you could do with a massage after pulling all those pints,' he would say. I'd shrug him off.

'Bet Paul could do with a massage,' I'd say. 'He's pulled more pints than me.'

'He has all those women fawning after him, why does he keep pestering me?' I asked Paul.

'Because you're pretty and you're clearly not interested in him,' he said. I blushed at the compliment.

'He's an old man,' I said, 'and he's married.'

About two weeks after a caesarean birth his wife arrived home. She was a 'bonnie girl' as we from the North would say, with brown curly hair and big trusting brown eyes. She was carrying a cute little baby girl.

Maurice was very attentive. He'd ordered flowers for her and chocolates. He helped her up the stairs to their living quarters. Perhaps he'll stop harassing me now, I thought.

A couple of nights later I was in the bar washing glasses. The pub was closed. I was alone as Paul had to leave early to meet his girlfriend. Maurice sneaked up behind me and brushed against me. Here we go again, I thought. He was stroking my hips. I lost it.

'Get off me,' I said as I pushed him away. 'You should be ashamed of yourself. You have a lovely wife and daughter upstairs.'

He grinned sheepishly.

'Maybe,' he replied. 'You are one of those girls who like to be wined and dined. Can I take you out?'

I couldn't believe what I was hearing, the audacity of the man. I was furious.

I don't have to put up with this, I thought.

'I'm giving you a week's notice starting from today,' I said.

'You don't have to take it that far,' he said. 'Besides, I don't have to pay you if you just walk out.'

'I'm not walking out. I'm giving you notice.'

For the first time since I'd worked there I felt in control. I didn't need to humour him anymore or put up with his silly sexual innuendoes or constant attempts to fondle me.

'I'd better not tell my boyfriend,' I said. 'He would go mad.'

'What boyfriend?' he asked. 'I've never seen you with anyone.'

'Oh, he works different shifts from me. He's a policeman.'

He stepped back. I became aware of someone coming out from the shadows. It was his wife and she was holding the baby. She'd crept downstairs and must have heard it all. She half smiled at me. 'Are you coming upstairs?' she said to Maurice.

Reluctantly, I turned up for work the next morning. Maurice kept well away from me and spoke only when it was necessary.

'What's up?' Paul asked. 'He's not hanging around you.'

'I've given him a week's notice,' I said.

'You are not leaving are you?'

I nodded.

'I'll miss you,' he said.

'You won't miss me nagging at you to help me out all the time.'

'Have you found another job?'

'No, not yet. The biscuit factory in Crumpsall is looking for packers. I'll try there.'

'My girlfriend was looking through the job advertisements in the Manchester Evening News. There were jobs advertised for usherettes, no experience needed. I've still got the advert. I'll bring it in tomorrow.'

'Ah thanks! You've been a great help to me. I hope I find a boyfriend as nice as you,' I told him.

Paul blushed.

I continued to serve out my notice and had only two more days to go. It was a quiet evening in the bar. I was pulling a pint for one of the regulars when I heard someone say, 'Hiya, gorgeous.'

I looked up and was astonished to see Faye standing at the bar. She'd had a drink. I was so distracted that I over filled the glass and it was spilling out over the brim.

'Who's that?' Paul asked as he handed me another glass. 'She's right butch looking isn't she?'

'It's Faye, she has a bedsit in the same house as me. I hope she doesn't cause a scene.'

'I'll have a double whiskey,' she shouted to Paul. 'Where's this Maurice?'

'He's downstairs,' Paul said as he hurried to get her a drink.

'Faye, what are you doing here?' I asked

She winked at me through glazed eyes. 'Just leave this to me,' she said.

Maurice came into the Bar.

'Are you the landlord?' she asked.

'Yes, I am,' he said politely.

She looked around. 'It's a nice place, is this. It's alright. I've never been in here before.' Faye could turn on the charm when she wanted to.

'I know you, Maurice,' she winked. She stretched out her arm for a handshake. Hesitantly, he shook it.

'Do I know *you*?' He asked, surprised at her familiarity.

'Not intimately,' she grinned. 'You're the wrong sex.' Maurice frowned.

'Ooh, I've heard all about *you*,' she said. 'You've got a reputation as a bit of a Casanova.'

'Have I?' he looked puzzled.

'Yeah. You have wives and girlfriends galore yet you can't get no satisfaction. Have you ever fancied turning queer?' His jaw dropped.

'Not likely,' he said.

The man that I had served a few minutes ago was listening. He spluttered on his beer.

Paul was grinning. I was holding my breath. *What was Faye going to say next?* I had no idea that she would be coming to see Maurice.

'I'd like a word with you,' Faye said to him. 'Can we go somewhere quiet?' She beckoned me over. 'Anne, you'd better come too.'

'What's going on?' Paul whispered.

'Faye's up to something,' I said.

I looked at Maurice. I was expecting him to say something but he didn't utter a word.

We moved away from the bar.

'I'm a friend of Anne's,' Faye said. 'I've heard she's having to leave because you're groping her all the time. I think she's entitled to compensation, don't you?' Maurice's jaw dropped for a second time. He looked at me, then back at Faye.

'And we've got witnesses.'

Have we? I wondered.

Faye went on, 'My Jo has friends in high places. One of 'em's a judge. If you come up before him he'll throw the book at you.'

I lost track of the rest of what she was saying. *One of Jo's gentlemen friends was a judge? Bloomin heck!*

'She could finish today,' I heard Maurice say, 'after she has done her shift. I'll pay her for the rest of the week.'

'Is that ok with you, Anne?' Faye asked. 'It will give you time to look for another job.'

She was certainly pulling the shots.

'Er, yeah,' I said.

'That wasn't too bad, was it?' she said to Maurice. 'I know you have a wife and a new baby to keep. You're probably a very nice man, just oversexed. You should have a word with Jo.'

Then she had the cheek to stretch out her hand and surprisingly Maurice shook it.

'What was all that about?' Paul said when I got back behind the bar.

'Don't ask,' I said. 'I think I'm in shock.'

USHERETTE

I returned to the pub the following evening to pick up my wages. Maurice was not around. Whether or not he was avoiding me, I don't know. He had left my wages at the bar with Paul. True to his word, he had paid me for an extra two days.

'Here's your wages,' Paul said, 'and here's the advert for the usherette. Good luck, I'll miss you.'

'I'll miss you too,' I said and I meant it.

I didn't waste any time. I went to the cinema right away. I was introduced to Marjorie, the supervisor. She looked about fifty.

'Have you had any experience?' she asked.

'None at all, but I'm willing to learn.'

'There's not much to it, really. It's just common sense. You can be trained on the job. Can you start tomorrow?'

'Yes.'

'Be here by eleven o' clock.'

That was that. I had walked out of one job and straight into another. It had been so easy, but jobs were ten a penny in the sixties.

The next day I turned up at the cinema on time. Marjorie took me to the staff room and introduced me to the other employees, who were sat around a table.

'This is Ethel, our longest serving usherette,' she said as she introduced me to a slim white-haired woman.

'I'm Norma,' another girl said, as she stubbed out a cigarette into an ash tray. 'You'll soon get the hang of it.'

'This is Diane, she's the cashier. And there's Carol and Babs, the ice cream girls. We're a friendly lot here,' she said.

Norma handed me a maroon overall. 'Try this on for size,' she said. All eyes were on me. I felt embarrassed. I put it on but it went way past my mini skirt.

'It's a bit long,' she said.

'She'll grow into it,' Ethel said.

Norma laughed. 'I think she's stopped growing by now. How old are you?' she asked.

'Eighteen.'

'You can grow until your twenty one,' Ethel said.

'I hope not,' I said.

Norma looked me up and down. 'I'll find her one that fits,' she said.

Soon I was donned out in a better fitting overall and I felt more like one of the group.

'Ethel will take you under her wing,' Marjorie said.

'All girls to their posts,' Marjorie shouted and soon I was stood in the foyer waiting for the doors to open. The stale smell of musty carpets and cigarette smoke reminded me of the Globe in Stockton. The nuns had taken us there to see a pantomime starring Frank Ifield. We had even seen Cliff Richard and The Shadows there. *Fond memories!*

The doors opened and the patrons came rushing in. It was like a buffalo stampede. I was tempted to just move out of their way.

Ethel stood her ground. She had it under control.

'Form an orderly queue,' she said. 'Get back in line,' she shouted to a couple of lads who tried to push in.

Ethel took it all in her stride. She efficiently tore half their tickets and returned the other half to them.

'We call this the gold rush,' she said, 'then you'll get the stragglers.

'Don't let me see you out of your seat,' she said to one lad who'd sauntered in.

'I won't, Miss'

'Promise?' Ethel said.

He grinned. 'Yes, Miss.'

'Go on in, then.'

She whispered to me, 'I'll need to check the doors at the side of the stage. They try to sneak their friends in.'

When the rush had died down, we sat in the foyer and took the tickets from the latecomers.

'If the picture has already started,' Ethel said, 'we use a torch to guide them to their seats.'

In the interval Diane and Babs the ice-cream girls walked up and down the aisle selling tubs of ice-cream and choc-ices.

I soon became part of the team. I enjoyed coming to work. I got to see lots of different films for free. Although not in one go as I was in and out of the cinema taking tickets and showing people to their seats.

One of my favourite films was *The son's of Katie Elder* starring John Wayne and Dean Martin. I was never one for the soppy romantic films. *Gone with the*

Wind was far too long, I thought. When the Beatles *A Hard Day's Night* was shown, it was standing room only.

If there was a particular film that I wanted to see I would stay back after my shift had finished to watch it.

One film was called *The Mystery and the Pleasure*. We had a line of men waiting to see that one. They must have thought it sounded erotic but it was about animals giving birth. They left the cinema in droves. 'That was disgusting,' they complained. 'They should give us our money back.'

There were the usual regulars, the men who would come after they had been on the booze. They would fall asleep and we had to wake them up when the film had finished.

Norma was one of the usherettes. She was in her late thirties and married. Her husband was a garage mechanic.

She was not shy when it came to talking about her sex life. She said her frequent headaches were due to the contraceptive pill. She had wanted her husband to get sterilised but he was too scared.

'You should have made him do without,' Ethel said.

'My doctor was totally against giving me the pill,' she said. 'Turns out he was a Catholic and it was against his principles. He suggested I use the rhythm method.'

'A rhythm method? What's that?' I asked. 'It sounds like a dance.' They all laughed.

'It's what they call natural family planning,' Norma explained. 'You avoid the days you can become pregnant or use condoms.'

But, both methods had failed her. 'That's why I've got five kids,' she said.

Norma went on to tell me that in 1961 she found out women were entitled to ask for the pill. From her, I learnt that women had a better chance of getting the pill if they told their doctor that having kids would be detrimental to their physical or mental health.

'I told my doctor straight that I'd crack up if I had any more kids!' she joked.

I learnt so much from Norma, in her crude way, about the facts of life.

THE BACK ROW

Ethel was getting on a bit and had been widowed a long time. She had been an usherette for as long as she could remember. Norma would tease her.

'You must have watched loads of the silent movies. Bet you fainted when Valentino came on the screen.'

'Ooh, yer cheeky monkey,' she would say.

Fred was a widower. He came to the cinema often as he had retired. He would arrive early so that he could sit in his favourite seat in the stalls. Ethel had time for him and they were always discussing the latest goings on in Coronation Street. We all thought he came in the cinema especially to see Ethel, but she insisted that were just friends. 'I knew his wife,' she'd say.

Marjorie told him it was Ethel's birthday and persuaded him to ask her out. She refused at first but we egged her on. 'Oh, go on Ethel,' Norma said. 'You only live once. He's lonely.' We usherettes agreed.

'Ethel, are you not lonely too?' I asked.

'Of course not, I have my job.'

Ethel had no children. She would have welcomed kids, but she couldn't have them and said it wasn't meant to be. She was so patient and she'd have been a good mother. Ethel lived in a terraced house and her best friend was called Doris. They were both members of the local Methodist church. She always seemed to be knitting something for the jumble sale and would often bring her knitting in. Although she could have gone up in rank she was not ambitious and said she preferred to be part of the team. She had known Marjorie for about ten years and showed her the ropes when she was a newcomer. The other staff teased her about Fred and she got embarrassed. 'Gerraway,' she'd say, but we sensed that she had a soft spot for him.

Janice was eighteen and she lived at home with her mam and stepfather and her younger brother and sister. We would catch the same bus to work in the morning.

'I'm envious,' she said when I told her that I shared a bedsit with a friend. 'I'd love to move out of our cramped house. I have to share a bedroom with my little sister.'

'Well, I still have to share a room.'

'Yes, but you can talk about boys and stuff like that. All my little sister wants to do is play with her dolls. Mind you, she's only five.'

Janice had a boyfriend. It was sort of on and off as he liked to go out with his mates a lot and she only saw him on certain days. She didn't think it would come to anything and it wasn't a serious relationship. She had known him from school. She liked the Beatles and had worked at the cinema six months longer than me.

'I love working here,' she said, 'but the hours play havoc with me love life.'

Marjorie was our supervisor. She was quite plump with dyed blonde curly hair. She was always smartly dressed and made up with red polished nails and lipstick to match. Her husband would drop of her off at the entrance door and much to her annoyance be waiting to pick her up at the end of her shift.

61

Once on my way in I saw her get out of the car and slam the door shut. She must have had an argument with him, I thought. Another time I overheard her complaining to Ethel. 'He's smashed the place up again,' she said, wiping her eyes. 'The bad tempered git.'

'Marjorie doesn't seem too happy,' I said to Norma. We were in the staff room having a cup of tea before opening time.

I had been working as an usherette for about three weeks. 'I'm not surprised,' Norma said, 'living with that brute.

Does he beat her up? I wondered. Somehow, I couldn't see this confident, well-dressed woman as being a battered wife.

'She wants a divorce, but he won't give her one.'

'Maybe he still loves her.'

'He has a fine way of showing it. Anyway, there's someone else.' Norma lowered her voice. 'Marjorie's having an affair,' she said.

'Is she?' I'm surprised.

'We have to be careful. Her husband's dead jealous and possessive.'

'What do you mean, *we* have to be careful?'

'Well Marj can't meet him outside, so he's comes here. They usually have a snogging session in the back row of the stalls. I don't know how she gets away with it. He must suspect something.'

Norma wasn't the only one who knew of the affair. All the other staff and even the cleaning ladies knew. They encouraged it. They didn't like her bad tempered husband one bit.

'He looks at you as if you were the dirt on his shoe,' Alma, one of the cleaners told me. So they were pleased that Marj, as they called her, was getting her own back.

I got a shock when I saw Marjorie's 'Romeo' for the first time. His name was George and he must have been over sixty. That seemed ancient to me.

He was bald, had a moustache and a paunch that would not have looked out of place at an antenatal clinic.

'He's a gentleman,' Norma said, when I joked that he wasn't exactly a Sean Connery.

It seemed that there was a conspiracy of silence to cover up for her. A warning procedure was in place if her husband turned up unexpectedly. If Diane the cashier saw him she would tell the girl on the sweet stall, who would then inform Ethel, who in turn would go into the cinema and warn Marjorie that her bad tempered husband was at the door. Marjorie would then scarper to the loo.

Ethel was a widow and lived alone. She quite enjoyed Marjorie's escapades and participated with relish in covering up for her. After one such incident in between taking tickets she said, 'I love coming to work, it's hilarious.'

One day Marjorie's husband turned up. He didn't stop to ask for his wife as he normally did. We wondered if he suspected something. The cashier was busy in the ticket kiosk serving customers. The girl usually on the sweet counter had gone to the loo. The early warning was lost. Ethel spotted him, but couldn't leave her post. She called me over and told me to go and warn Marjorie.

I grabbed my torch and went into the auditorium. It was dark and I struggled to make my way through a fog of smoke from countless cigarettes. I switched the torch on and directed it at the stairs so I could see where I was going.

I expected Marjorie and George to be in the rear seats so I shone the torch on the people sitting in the back row. There was a scrambling as lovers adjusted their clothing.

'Fuck off, what you're playing at?' one young lad said.

I couldn't find them. *Where were they?* I was starting to panic. I shone the torch across the back seats. All eyes followed the direction of my torch. At last I spotted them, but couldn't get across to warn of the danger. They were sat in the corner, locked in a passionate embrace. His hand was up her skirt, showing her plump white thighs. George looked up. I don't know who got the bigger shock; him, Marjorie or me. I nearly dropped the torch.

'Don't ever do that again,' she said to me afterwards. 'I know you meant well, but George nearly had a heart attack and you frightened the life out of me.'

They were much more discreet after that.

THE LETTER

I was in my bedsit when there was a knock on the door. I opened it and saw that it was Faye.

'Come in,' I said. 'It makes a change you coming to our room. It's the first time you've been in here since we moved in.'

'It were a right messy room when Lackey lived here,' she said, looking around. 'Ee, it's all clean and tidy now.'

'Do you want a cuppa?'

'Nah, I'm not staying long,' she said.

She went over to the window and stood there for a while puffing hard on a cigarette. She was about to speak but changed her mind.

I got the feeling that she wanted to tell me something.

'What is it, Faye?' I asked.

She turned round. 'You know I really like you.'

'Ah, we're not going down that road,' I thought.

'You know I'm always making a pass at ya, but it's all in good fun,' she said.

I laugh. 'I take it all in good fun.'

'I love Jo,' Faye said.

'I know you do, you'd be lost without her. And she looks after you. You're just a randy old fellow making a pass at a young piece.'

She grinned. 'Cheek, I'm only in me thirties.'

'That's ancient,' I said. 'I'm only eighteen.'

She sat in the armchair and flicked ash into the ashtray.

'I've come to ask you a favour,' she said looking down at the carpet.

'What is she about to ask me?' I wonder.

'I'd like you to write a letter for me,' she said.

'A letter?'

'Yeah.'

'Who to?'

'Me son.'

'Your son?'

'Yeah,' she nodded. 'It's his birthday next week and I'd like to send him some money.'

Faye has a son? I was surprised.

She reached into her pocket for her wallet and took out a photograph. 'That's him,' she said as she handed it to me.

It was a black and white photo of a good looking lad with dark hair and eyes. He looked like Faye.

'He's the spit of you,' I said. 'He's gorgeous.'

Faye grinned. 'So, you think he's gorgeous like me do ya?'

I blushed bright red. 'I meant to say he…'

'I know what you meant,' she said laughing. 'Ooh, I thought you were making a pass at me then.'

'Behave yourself, Faye,' I said, mimicking Jo.

Earlier, I had written a letter to my sister and the writing pad was on the table. I sat down and turned over the page.

'Right then, what do you want me to write?'

'Dunno,' she said.

'What's his name?' I ask.

'Karl. It's spelt with a K.'

66

'That's a nice name. Unusual. Do you want me to put this address down?'

'Fuck no! No way, don't want the old bird turning up here and causing trouble.'

'The old bird?'

'Me mother.'

I wrote, 'Dear Karl,' then asked, 'What would you like me to say?'

'I don't know how to put it, really.'

'Well, you tell me what you'd like to say to him and I'll put it into words.'

'OK,' she nodded. I could sense that this was quite emotional for her.

'Do you see him often?' I asked.

'Nah, not as much as I'd like. He lives with me mother in Oldham.'

'How old is he?'

'Coming up thirteen.'

'He'll be a teenager, then,' I said.

She nodded. 'I don't go home too often. It causes rows with the old bird. It upsets the lad. She always nags at me to dress properly, but you can't help what you are, can you?'

'Has she met Jo?'

'Yeah, just the once, she ignored her.'

'How sad.'

'I couldn't take Jo home, she'd have a fit.'

'How long have you and Jo been together?'

'Seven years.'

'Seven years? Ooh, you'll have to be careful.'

'Why?' she asked, wrinkling her forehead.

'*The Seven Year Itch* was showing in our cinema the other week. People get itchy feet after seven years together and start messing about. Marilyn Monroe was in it.'

'I wouldn't mind messing about with her,' she grinned.

'I think we could start with Happy Birthday,' I said, changing the subject.

'Karl loves football,' she said. 'He's a Manchester United Fan. I'm sending him money so he can buy their football kit. Thinks Georgie Best is a brilliant footballer, he's his hero.'

'Yeah, he's good looking is Georgie,' I said. 'I've been in the Best Boutique. It costs a fortune though, to buy clothes in there. Over priced I think.'

'I'm also thinking of getting Karl a ticket for the Man U match,' she said. 'It'd be a surprise. He'd love it. But I'm dreading telling Jo.'

'Why?'

'Well, I'd like him to stay over at our bedsit but she'd have to move out for the night.'

'Couldn't he sleep on the settee?'

'It's not that. He doesn't know that me and Jo are a couple.'

'Why don't you tell him?'

She sighed. 'I couldn't, he'd get upset. Me sister was having an argument with me mother about me and Jo. I don't know what she said but Karl overheard and got upset. 'Faye's not queer,' he said. That's what I'm up against.'

I wondered if her sister had been telling the truth, or what if this was just a ploy to get Faye back home.

68

'I think they're trying to break you and Jo up,' I said. 'They're making you feel guilty.'

'Don't I know it,' she said as she stubbed out a cigarette.

'Better tell the old bird that I'll send her some money. Put that in the letter, will ya, that'll cheer her up.'

'*I'll be sending the old bird some money,* is that what you want me to say?' I joked.

'Bloody 'ell. Don't write that! It'd make Karl laugh though.'

'He must share your sense of humour,' I said.

'Yeah, he's a lot like me,' she said.

When I had finished the letter I asked Faye to sign her name, and then I put it in an envelope and handed it to her.

That was the easy part. Now Faye would have to decide between Jo and her son. That was going to be difficult.

LIAM

'Where are you off to then?' I said to Liam.

He was coming down the stairs as I was going up to my bedsit after an evening shift at the cinema. It was after eleven at night.

'I'm off to paint the town red,' he replied.

'There was a man looking for you earlier on. He went up to your room. He didn't seem very happy that you weren't in.'

'Oh that was Robbie,' Liam said as he crinkled his nose. 'I'm avoiding him.'

'How's the new job going?'

'I love it! The staff are great and I get to see loads of films. *Zorba the Greek* is on next week. Faye's asked me to get two tickets for her and Jo.'

'I heard that Faye went in the pub and sorted Pervy out.'

'She did. I nearly died when I saw her at the bar, but she did me a favour. I bumped into the barman the other day. He told me Maurice reckons I'm a queer.'

'That's because I wanted nothing to do with him. Honestly, that man thinks he's God's gift to women!'

'And I'm God's gift to men,' Liam laughed.

There was a knock on the front door and Liam rushed down to open it. It was his friend Dean.

'Taxi's waiting, let's go!' said Dean. The front door slammed shut after them and I went into my room.

Katie was sat up in bed reading. 'I told Liam that a man was looking for him,' I said to her. 'He says it was Robbie but he's avoiding him. I wonder why?'

'He couldn't wait for him to get out of prison,' Katie replied.

'Anyway, he's married with kids. He shouldn't be messing about,' I said. 'I don't know how a man can have sex with both a man and a woman. Tania told me what a bisexual is. I'd never heard of it.'

'She knows everything, that Tania,' Katie said. 'I just hope she knows how to keep herself safe.'

I made a cup of tea and got into bed. 'How's it going at Marshall Ward?'

'It's ok. Some of the girls are having a night out on Saturday. They asked me to go with them.'

'Are you going?'

'I was thinking about it, thought you might like to come with us?'

'I can't, I'm working.'

'Can't you get out of it?'

'No, Marjorie's already done the rota. I don't want to let her down. You should go, though, and have a good time. You might meet someone nice.'

'I thought my last boyfriend was nice until I found out that he was a bloody two timer.'

'Paul's nice, you know the barman at the pub? I like him, pity he's courting.'

'By the way, you know that girl at our work? The one who's pregnant? She's showing now. Her mam thinks she's just putting on weight. I reckon she's going to have to tell her sooner or later. She says if her dad finds out he'll make her have an abortion.'

'She can't have an abortion,' I said. 'It's a sin.'

'A sin?'

'It's something the nuns taught us when I was in Nazareth House. It would be a mortal sin to kill a baby.'

'She can't have one now, anyway. It would be too risky. She's six months gone'.

I switched the light off and lay on my bed. There was the usual slamming of doors as the other tenants came in, but I soon dropped off to sleep. I was awoken by a gentle rapping on our door. At first I thought I was hearing things, as Katie hadn't stirred.

I listened intently and there it was again. Then, someone called my name. It wasn't particularly dark in the room so I didn't switch the light on. I got out of bed and went over to the door.

'Who is it?' I said.

'It's me, Liam. Hurry up and let me in!'

I quickly turned the key in the lock and opened the door.

Liam came barging in.

'Lock the door,' he said. I turned the key in the lock. Katie woke up.

'What's going on?' She asked.

'Can I hide in here? Robbie's looking for me. He'll kill me if he finds me. If he knocks on your door, don't open it.'

His hands were shaking as he took a cigarette out of a packet. 'Have you got a light?'

I went over to the stove picked up a box of matches and handed them to him. His hands were trembling so much that I took a match out of the box and lit his cigarette.

'You really are scared,' I said.

'I'm terrified,' he said. 'When he's had a drink, he's a maniac.'

Now he had me scared.

'The last time he beat me up I ended up in hospital.'

'Oh my God,' I said. 'I think we should put the armchair in front of the door.'

Katie jumped out of bed. The three of us carried the armchair and put it in front of the door.

Liam was still shaking. I took a blanket and put it over his shoulders. I could smell the alcohol on his breath.

'Sit on my bed,' I said. 'Does he know you've come back here?'

'No, but he will definitely come here looking for me'.

'If he knocks on our door asking for you, I'll tell him you're not here,' I said.

'Me too,' Katie said.

We heard the front door opening. Liam gave a sharp intake of breath. My heart was racing. With bated breath we waited for the footsteps to come pounding up the stairs.

We heard a door closing.

'It's one of the tenants,' Katie whispered. 'It must be Dougie.' There was a sigh of relief but it was short lived.

It must have been about twenty minutes later when we heard footsteps coming up the pathway.

I got up and stood back from the window so I wouldn't be seen from the outside. I peeped through the curtains.

'It's him,' I said. 'Does he have a key, Liam?

'No.'

'Thank God for that, he won't be able to get in.'

'Unless some idiot hasn't locked the front door,' Katie said.

No sooner had she spoken the front door was flung open. The riffraff had arrived.

Footsteps came charging up the stairs. They didn't stop at our floor but went up above us to Liam's room.

An almighty bang was heard.

'He's bust the door in,' Liam said.

We could hear the splintering of glass.

'That's my record collection,' he sighed.

'He's on the rampage,' I said. 'I hope he doesn't start banging on the old man's door.'

I'd passed him on the stairs a few times since he'd come home from the hospital. I'd said a cheery hello to him but he hadn't responded, just given me a blank stare.

'He's still traumatised from his war experience,' Faye said.

Footsteps came thundering down the stairs. They stopped at Tania's door. There was a loud knocking on her door. Does this man have no consideration, I thought, waking people up in the middle of the night?

'She's not in,' Katie whispered. 'She's staying over in Moss Side tonight.'

The footsteps arrived at our door. All three of us froze. There was a loud banging on the door. 'Has anyone seen Liam?' he asked. We looked at each other.

'Don't answer,' Liam whispered.

There was another loud knock on our door.

'I'll tell him we haven't seen you, then he'll leave us alone,' I whispered.

'Who is it?' I shouted.

'I'm looking for Liam, have you seen him?'

'No I haven't,' I said, with all the confidence that I could muster.

We heard Faye and Jo's door opening.

'What's up, Robbie?' Faye asked.

'I'm looking for that fucking skinny runt Liam. I'll kill him if I get my hands on him.'

'Why, what's he done?' Faye asked.

'That's between him and me.'

'Come in and have a cuppa,' she said. 'I know you're upset, but he won't be in there with the lasses.'

Robbie was still effing and blinding when he went in her room. Faye was making sympathetic noises. We heard the door close.

'Good old Faye,' Katie whispered. 'She is trying to calm him down.'

We didn't dare move. Our senses were heightened as we listened out for every sound coming from Faye's room.

Liam and I were sat on my single bed, our heads against the pillow. He was so close that I could almost taste the alcohol on his breath. In the dim light he looked ghostly pale. I patted him on his bony knee.

'Don't worry, we won't let him get you,' I said. To lighten the mood I added, 'Katie and me will hit him over the head if we have to.'

Robbie seemed to be spending ages talking to Faye and Jo. At last we heard the door to their room opening. We held our breath. Robbie went down the stairs much more quietly than he'd come up them. He closed the front door behind him.

'Good riddance,' Katie said.

The early morning light was shining through the curtains and I was weary.

'We'd better get some sleep,' I said. I looked over at Liam. He was falling asleep. I didn't want to disturb him, so Katie gave me one of her blankets. I sat in the armchair and wrapped the blanket around me. Thoughts were going through my head. *What had Liam done to make Robbie want to kill him? And why had he beaten him so badly in the past that he'd ended up in hospital?* Liam should have nothing to do with this maniac, I thought. It was as simple as that.

But I had never been in love and I didn't understand the complexities involved.

I must have dozed off as I was awoken by a knock on the door. I jumped up.

'Who is it?' I shouted. Katie and Liam awoke.

'It's me, Faye. Tell Liam Robbie's gone home. He went hours ago.'

I grinned. Faye had known all along that he'd been in our room.

'Open the door,' she said. 'We want to talk to Liam.'

'Hold on, Faye, I'll just move the armchair from the door.'

'They've barricaded themselves in,' I heard her saying to Jo.

'You can open the door now,' Faye said, 'the cavalry's here.'

AFTERMATH

'He's tolerable when he's sober, but a bad un when he's had a drink,' Faye said. 'He's a Jekyll and Hyde.'

We were sat in her bedsit. It was the morning after Robbie had gone on the rampage looking for Liam. Katie and I were sat on the ottoman drinking tea. Liam was in the armchair, pale faced, hands trembling and smoking a cigarette.

'How did you know Liam was in our room, Faye?' I asked.

'I heard Liam knocking on your door and calling out your name. I was going to tell him to come in our room if you hadn't answered. I had a feeling that Robbie was on the warpath.'

'Why, has it happened before?' Katie asked.

Faye looked at Liam. She nodded. 'Many times,' she said.

'That old man must have been terrified,' Jo said. 'Liam, you really have to do something about Robbie.'

'What if the old man had opened his door?' I said.

'He wouldn't have,' Faye said. 'He doesn't open his door for anybody but Mrs Lowe. He would have thought it was the Gestapo.'

'I know. I feel real guilty about it,' Liam said.

'Why don't you finish with Robbie?' I said 'Tell him you don't love him anymore.'

'It's not as easy as that,' Liam replied.

There was a knock on the door. It was Mrs Lowe. She came into the room.

'Well, well,' she said. 'That's a fine mess he's made of your room, Liam, not to mention the door.'

Liam sighed. He looked as if he was about to burst into tears.

'I'll pay for it to be fixed, Mrs Lowe, honestly I will.'

'You certainly will,' she said.

She went over to him and patted his shoulder. 'Well, I suppose those things can be replaced, but you can't,' she said.

'Would you like a cuppa, Mrs Lowe?' Jo asked.

Mrs Lowe nodded. 'I could do with something stronger,' she said, 'after I've seen the damage done to my house.'

'How's the old man?' Jo asked.

'He's alright,' Mrs Lowe said. 'Thankfully, he's all right.

'But, if you want to stay in my house, Liam, we may have to move you downstairs. We have to think of Jacob.'

She turned to Katie and me. 'I heard that you hid him in your room. You must have been frightened?'

'We were scared stiff,' Katie said.

'But we were more terrified for Liam,' I added.

'I'm really sorry for putting you through all that,' Liam said.

I became concerned that if he thought it was too much bother he might be afraid to ask us for help.

'If it ever happens again,' I said, 'you can knock on our door anytime.'

'What do you mean, if it happens again?' Mrs Lowe said. 'I hope that this is the end of it because if it does happen again I'll have to call the police. I can't have a mad man running riot through my house.'

There was a knock on the door. 'It's me, Dougie.'

Jo opened the door. 'Come in,' she said.

'I've come to apologise to Liam,' Dougie said. 'I went up to his room but fucking hell it's a mess and the door's hanging off its hinges!' He spotted Mrs Lowe.

'Oops! Sorry for swearing Mrs Lowe!' he said.

'What have you got to apologise to Liam for?' she asked.

'It was me who left the front door unlocked. I was pissed.'

'It wouldn't have made any difference,' Faye said. 'He would have smashed that door in as well.'

'Do you know, Liam,' said Dougie, 'that he's broken your record player? Maybe he doesn't like your records.'

Liam half smiled.

Mrs Lowe rolled her eyes. 'I'd better be going. I need to get someone to fix the door.'

'I'll do it for you, Mrs. Lowe,' Dougie said. 'I know where I can get a door on the cheap.'

'Yes, I'm sure you do,' she said, 'but I have my own handyman.' She left the room.

'Liam, I can get you another record player,' Dougie said. 'You can have it for free. I didn't want Mrs Lowe to know, but I left the door unlocked for my girlfriend. She works in a nightclub and finishes late. I left it unlocked for her.'

'Why didn't you wait for her and come home together?' Jo asked.

'I had business to see to.'

'Summit to do with warehouses?' Faye asked.

'Not this time,' he said.

RITA

I got home from the cinema. It was pouring with rain. I was drenched through. Katie had gone out with the girls from work. They were going onto a nightclub so I was not expecting her back until the early hours of the morning. I plugged the one bar electric fire into the socket. I stripped my wet clothes off and put my baby doll nightie on.

I switched the radio on. The Beatles' *A Hard Day's Night* was playing. I'd just put the kettle on the stove when there was a knock on the door.

'Katie?' asked a voice. It was Dougie.

'Katie's not here, she's gone out for the night,' I said.

'There's someone downstairs. She's asking to see Katie,' he said.

I wondered who it could be. No one had called for Katie before.

I quickly put my dressing gown on and my slippers and I half opened the door.

'She's waiting at the bottom of the stairs,' he said. 'She's soaked through, poor thing.'

I came down the stairs and saw a young girl stood there soaking wet and shivering.

'I'm sorry but Katie's not in. She's gone out with the lasses from work,' I told her.

'Oh, I forgot,' she said. 'Will you tell her I called? Only she told me if I ever needed help to come round here. Katie gave me this address.'

She looked worried and turned to leave.

It suddenly dawned on me. 'Are you Rita?' I asked.
'Yes.'

'Katie has mentioned you,' I said.

I did not want to break Katie's confidence and tell her that I knew of her situation so I added, 'You're one of her mates from work, aren't you?' She nodded.

'Come on up, you can wait for her in our bedsit. It's a lousy night to be hanging about.'

We went into the bedsit.

'The kettle's boiling. Would you like a cuppa?'

'Yes please,' she said. 'I'd love one.'

She was dripping puddles onto the lino.

'Take your coat off,' I said. 'I'll try and dry it for you.'

She handed me her coat. It was obvious that she was pregnant. I put the coat over the chair in front of the electric bar, and placed a towel under it to catch the drips.

Rita sat in the armchair.

I gave her a cup of tea and put a few Jammie Dodgers on a plate.

'Katie won't be back 'til late. They are going onto a nightclub.'

I handed her a towel. Her hair was sopping wet and was dripping down her face. It was then that I noticed she'd been crying.

'Don't worry,' I said. 'We'll help you if we can.'

'Has Katie told you about me?'

'What is there to know?' I asked.

'I'm nearly seven months pregnant. I'm not married. The father doesn't want to know and I'm in deep shit,' she said. 'My mum thought I was putting on the weight.

'I tried to hide it from her but I've got so big. In the end she guessed. It must have been playing on her mind because as soon as I got in from work she demanded to know. She asked me if the boyfriend knew.

'When I told her I'd found out he was married she went ballistic. She told me dad. He wanted me to have an abortion but I'm too far gone for that. He went berserk and he was throwing things around. He's got a right temper on him, 'as me dad. We had one hell of a row. Then he told me to get of the house. He threw me out.'

'What?' I said. 'He threw you out in this weather.' She nodded.

'It was awful. He called me a slut and said he didn't want any bastard kid in his house.'

'But this bairn will be his grandchild,' I said.

I wondered how any parent could just abandon their own flesh and blood. Then it occurred to me that my mother had abandoned me and I hadn't been an adult, I had been a two-year-old child.

I felt sorry for her.

'You can stay here tonight,' I said.

'Are you sure?'

'Definitely, I can't let you go out in this weather. Besides, if you go back home he might hit you.'

'Ah thanks, I've got nowhere else to go. I suppose I could go to me auntie's but she lives miles away.'

We sat there in silence then she said.

'You're Anne, aren't you?

'Yes.'

'Katie told me that you both come from the North East and that you share a bedsit.'

'Do you know,' I said, 'we've only been in Manchester for four months, and yet it seems like ages ago. My eyes have certainly been opened!

'I feel as though I was living on another planet. I was sweet and innocent before I came here!'

'So were I before I met him.'

'Does his wife know about you?'

'I think so. He told me she does. But she's standing by him.'

'I would have flung him out,' I said

'Don't think she'll do that.'

'Why not?'

'She's pregnant too.'

'Crikey.'

Rita looked around the bedsit.

'What's it like, living here in this house?'

'Mad at times. Me and Katie keep saying we're going to look for another bedsit but we can't seem to get round to it.'

'I've heard it's full of queers, prostitutes and thieves,' Rita said.

'Who told you that?'

'Dunno, can't remember now.'

'I suppose it is,' I laughed. 'But when Katie and I moved in here we were skint and they helped us out. They're not a bad lot really.'

'Me dad hates queers. He says they should be shot'.

And this coming from a man who would kill his own grandchild, I thought.

84

In the background the radio was playing *I won't Live in a World without Love*, by Peter and Gordon.

'I like this song,' she said. 'It's quite sad, though.'

I moved the chair further back from the fire because there was steam coming of her coat.

'Are you warm enough?'

She nodded.

'You can sit on Katie's bed, you'll be more comfortable,'

'I will, if you don't mind, me back's killing me.'

When Katie came back in the early hours she found Rita fast asleep on her bed.

'I had a great night,' Katie said the next morning, 'and I've met a fella. He's asked me out. We're thinking of going to the pictures next Saturday to see the latest James Bond film.'

'Just make sure he isn't married. Don't find out too late like I did,' Rita said.

'No, he's free and single. It's Pauline's brother, you know her from admin. She was out with us. She'd have told us if he was married. We bumped into him in the pub.

'His name's Jeff and he's gorgeous. He had another lad with him. Do you fancy making a foursome Anne?'

'I don't know. What if I don't like him?'

'You could make an excuse and disappear.'

'How am I going to do that? I'm not Genie of the lamp.'

Rita went into Cheetham Village to ring her mother and try and gauge the situation at home. She knew her father wouldn't let her go back home, not with a baby in tow. She needed to speak to her mother though ask her advice.

Katie and I sat on our beds eating toast.

'What's Rita going to do if he won't let her go home?' I said. 'How's she going to manage?'

'Where's she going to live?' Katie asked.

The questions bounced between us, but we both knew we wouldn't see her on the streets.

'I know,' I said. 'We'll ask Faye. She'll know what to do.'

When Rita came back she was in tears. 'Me mam's told me to stay away. She said me dad was ranting and raving all night. He's blaming her. He's said she spoilt me by giving me too much freedom.'

'That's ridiculous,' Katie said. 'What was she supposed to do? Lock you up?'

'I feel awful. I've got *them* arguing now. Maybe I should have had an abortion.'

'You don't mean that,' I said.

'Surely they'll feel different when the baby's here,' Katie said.

I was sceptical. 'Don't count on it,' I said.

I'd seen many a baby given up for adoption in Nazareth House. *Where were the grandparents of these little ones? Had they abandoned them too?*

'I've got nowhere to go,' she said. 'I'll have to look for digs.'

'Not in your condition,' Katie said. 'You won't stand a chance.'

'You can stay with us for now,' she said. 'You don't mind, do you, Anne?'

'Of course not, but we'll have to hide you from Mrs Lowe. And just one thing, Rita, don't have the baby in here. I know how to look after newly born babies, I've had plenty of experience, but please don't ask me to deliver it!'

Katie and I took it in turns to sleep in the armchair. Rita slept in the bed. We insisted.

'You need your sleep,' we would tell her. She was still working at Marshall Ward and would go into work with Katie. We knew that this would only be a temporary solution. Soon she would have to find a place for her and the baby.

I took Rita to Faye and Jo's bedsit and introduced her.

They knew all about Rita's situation. Katie had told them.

'This is Rita,' I said.

'Come in,' Faye said. 'Sit yourself in the armchair, chucks, you'll be more comfy.'

'Put your feet up an' all,' she said as she plonked a foot stool at Rita's feet.

'Have you had owt to eat?'

'Yes,' Rita replied shyly.

'Make her a cup of char, Jo.'

'Would you like a biscuit?' Jo asked. 'You'd better have two one for the baby,' she smiled.

They were fussing over her like two mother hens.

There was a bemused look on Rita's face but I suspect she rather enjoyed it.

'I'll ask Mrs Lowe if she knows of any bedsits available,' Faye said, after Rita told them about her dilemma.

'You'll have to claim from the social an' all,' she said.

'Have you any clothes for the baby?' Jo asked.

'I've got nowt,' Rita said.

'I will have to get my knitting needles out then,' Jo said.

'Are Faye and Jo lesbos?' Rita asked when we got back to our bedsit.

'Whatever made you think that?' Katie asked.

'Well that Faye dresses like a fella and she's dead butch looking.'

Katie and I laughed.

'They're dead nice, though, aren't they?' Rita said.

RITA'S MAM

It was nine o'clock in the morning. I was listening to the radio and having a leisurely breakfast of tea and toast.

Katie and Rita had gone to work. I didn't have to be at the cinema until eleven. There was a knock on the front door. I ignored it. It's one of Dougie's mates, I thought. He's probably lying in bed after a late night. He didn't have a job. Well, not a lawful one, anyway. Let him answer it, I thought. But the knocking was persistent. I looked out of the window to see a woman staring up at me. Now she's seen me, I thought, I'd better go and find out what she wants.

I locked the door and went bounding down the stairs. A middle-aged woman was stood on the doorstep. She was an older version of her daughter.

'I'm Rita's mam,' she said. 'Is she in?'

'I'm sorry but she's at work,' I said.

'I've heard she's staying with a girl called Katie.'

'I share a bedsit with Katie. Rita's been staying with both of us. Shall I give her a message? You can come back after work and see her if you want.'

'I won't be able to,' she lowered her voice, 'her dad doesn't know I'm here.'

'Shall I tell her you called round, then?' I said. She turned to go, hesitated, and then came near to me.

'Try and persuade her to have the baby adopted will you?' she said before leaving.

I was stunned. I went back up the stairs in a daze. *Try and persuade her to have the baby adopted?* That might be what Rita's mother wanted. I suppose she saw that as a solution. But Rita hadn't mentioned anything about adoption. Persuade Rita to have the baby adopted? I'm blooming sure I won't!

I knocked on Faye's door and she opened it in her dressing gown.

'Come in,' she yawned. 'What time do you call this? We night owls need our beauty sleep. Who was that knocking at the front door? Woke us up, thought they'd never stop.'

I sat down in the armchair.

'It was Rita's mam. She wants me to try and persuade Rita to have the baby adopted.'

'Bloody 'ell,' Faye said, 'she doesn't ask for much, does she?'

'What does she want you to do?' Jo asked. She was putting rollers in her hair.

'To give her baby away to strangers,' I said.

In Nazareth House I remembered hearing about a young girl who was forced to give her baby up for adoption. She had screamed so much that they'd had to sedate her. I bet the whole experience scarred her for life. I didn't want that for Rita.

'I'm going to tell Rita that her mother called round. But, I'm not going to mention anything about adoption. I don't want to upset her,' I said.

'It may be for the best,' Jo said.

'Yeah, it could go to someone who couldn't have kids. They might be rich. It'd want for nothing then,' Faye said.

'Why does she have to give her baby away, anyway?' I said. I didn't see a problem. 'Rita's mother will probably come to accept the baby in time'.

'What about her dad?' Faye said. 'He won't accept it.'

'Why do men have to tell women what to do?' I said. '*They* don't go through the trauma of giving birth. I don't understand why Rita's mam won't stand up to him. There's no man going to tell *me* what to do.'

'Hark! Listen to her!' Faye said.

'Ooh, I pity the fella who gets you,' Jo said grinning.

'I'd bloody envy him,' Faye said.

'Behave yourself Faye,' Jo and I said together.

LIAM'S BEDSIT

I'd arrived back after shopping at Cheetham Hill. Liam had asked me to get him a packet of cigarettes. It had been a few days since the 'Robbie' incident. I went up to his bedsit. The door had been replaced. It was wide open. There were no records playing.

I knocked on the door. I would never just walk in without being asked.

'Come in,' he shouted.

I got a shock. One side of the wall was painted black. It seemed to make the room smaller and claustrophobic.

'Doesn't that wall make you depressed looking at it?' I asked.

'It suits my mood,' he said.

I hoped he wasn't going into one of his 'downers' as Faye called them. Apart from that episode with Robbie, I'd always found him to be upbeat and funny and constantly on the go.

'That's why you're so skinny,' I'd say.

He didn't seem to eat. He just drank cups of tea and smoked an endless number of cigarettes. Jo was always trying to get him to eat something. 'You need fattening up,' she would say, or, 'You'll fade away.' He'd told me that he'd come to Manchester from the South. He wanted to have the freedom to live as he wanted. He had met Robbie in prison. They had been cellmates. I didn't ask him why he had been in prison. He had not asked me about my background and we respected each other's privacy.

He had a vast record collection of both LPs and 45rpms. His taste in music ranged from the musicals and pop music to opera. Only a week ago I'd been sat in his bedsit when he told me that his favourite composer was Puccini.

'Who is Puccini?' I'd asked him.

'He composed some fantastic music,' Liam said. 'Listen to this.'

He'd put a long-playing record on the record player. We'd listened in silence. The music was just enchanting. I'd never really appreciated opera before. It was only for posh people, I'd thought.

'This is *Vissi di'arte*,' Liam said.

'It sounds Latin,' I said.

I was familiar with the language. When I'd been at the orphanage and we'd gone to church, the mass, benediction and even the hymns were all sung in Latin.

I wanted to impress Liam so I'd made the sign of the cross and said, 'In nomine patris et filii et spiritus sancti.'

His eyes widened.

'Amen,' he'd said. 'You know your Latin, don't you?'

'Did you know what I was saying?'

'Certainly do, I used to be an altar boy.'

'You weren't brought up by nuns or priests were you?' I'd asked

'No, I had a very happy upbringing,' he said.

I don't know why, but I'd been surprised.

I looked around the bedsit. Dougie had given him a record player as promised and Katie and I had clubbed together to buy him a record. *Don't let the Sun Catch you Crying* by *Gerry and the Pacemakers*. I thought it rather apt after his ordeal with Robbie.

Along with most of his record collection Robbie had smashed that nice Puccini one.

He has no taste in music I thought.

THERE'S THIEVES ABOUT

'**I**'ll kill the thieving, lying bastard,' Dougie shouted to Faye as he came down the stairs.

I was making my way up the stairs after nipping out to the shop for a pair of tights in the popular American tan shade. I needed them for work.

'I'll go and see Mrs Lowe,' he said. He stormed out slamming the front door behind him.

'What's all that about, Faye?' I asked. She was stood at the top of the stairs.

'That mate of his, Jimmy or whatever his name is, has done the dirty on him. He's run off with a stash of goods belonging to Dougie. Not only that, he broke into Mrs Lowe's house and stole her Jewish candelabra. Dougie's fuming about that.'

'Was Mrs Lowe in at the time?'

'Luckily she weren't. She were staying with her son in Blackley for the weekend. Dougie's gone round to see her.'

There was an unwritten law amongst the tenants. You could steal from your own mother but not Mrs Lowe. Whoever did would find themselves in a lot of bother.

'I wouldn't like to be in his shoes,' Tania said as she opened the door to her bedsit. 'I heard it all.'

'What did he steal from Dougie?' I asked Faye.

'Ah, just things that he'd nicked from the warehouse, but half of the hoard belongs to Scots Billy. Wait until he finds out. They'll be murder.'

Thieves stealing from each other, it seemed fair game to me, but Mrs Lowe was a different story.

'Where is Scots Billy anyway?' I asked. 'I haven't seen him for a while.'

Faye said she didn't know.

Dougie came in the front door. 'Come and have a cup of char, Dougie,' Faye shouted. 'How's Mrs Lowe?'

'Fuming, and I don't blame her. I mean that candlestick or whatever she calls it has religious significance for her. She's very upset. And I feel responsible because I brought the bastard here.'

So you should, I thought, bringing riffraff into the house.

We went into Faye's room. 'I'll just put the kettle on,' she said.

'Where's Jo?' I asked. There was no sign of her.

'She has gone to meet a gentlemen friend.'

I often wondered about these gentlemen friends. One was a judge, Faye had said, but I wasn't sure whether to believe her. Maybe she was only saying that to scare Maurice, I thought. I was curious about what exactly Jo did with them. I'd asked her once when she'd been inebriated and more than willing to tell us about her secret life.

'They're mostly older professional men,' she'd said. 'Some of them are married and just want to talk. Others just like me to undress them and play around with them.'

I didn't like to ask what she meant by 'play around with them'.

96

'There is one who is quite kinky, but he pays me a lot of money,' she said

'What do you think she means by kinky?' I'd asked Katie.

'He might like to be tied up.'

'Tied up, what for?'

'It's called bondage. Some men like a domineering woman who treats them like a slave.'

'A slave? We could do with one of those.'

'I've heard that they even get them to lick their boots,' Katie said.

'Now, that sounds kinky to me,' I'd said.

There was a knock on the door. 'Who is it?' Faye shouted.

'It's Billy,'

'Let him in,' Faye said. Dougie opened the door.

Scots Billy stormed into the room.

'What the fuck's going on, Dougie? Just heard that Jimmy Grant has nicked our loot.'

'He has! He was supposed to pick it up and bring it here but he's scarpered.'

'The bastard, I'll fucking kill him! Do you know where he hangs out?'

'The Snakepit. He was in there last night.'

'Where the fuck's that?'

'Piccadilly.'

'Right then, we'll go and find the bastard,' Scots Billy said and he made for the door.

'He broke into Mrs Lowe's and pinched her candelabra,' Faye said.

'What! He stole from the old woman? The bastard!'

'Mrs Lowe hasn't told the cops yet,' Dougie said. 'She doesn't want her son to know. He's always on at her about selling this house.'

Billy stormed out of the room as Dougie hurried behind trying to keep up with him.

'He swears a lot, doesn't he?' I said to Faye.

'I've yet to meet a Scotsman that doesn't,' she said.

BLIND DATE

'I've got nothing to wear,' Katie said. 'I wonder if Tania will lend me a dress. I'll go and ask her.' It was early evening on a Saturday. We were getting ready to go out. Katie had nagged me into making up a foursome.

'His name's Colin,' she said. 'You'll like him'. That was the only information I had about my blind date.

We were meeting them in The Empress pub on Cheetham Hill Road. That suited me. I didn't want to be too far from home in case Colin and I didn't hit it off.

I wore my new mini dress and kitten heel shoes. I tied my long hair back with a black velvet band. I sprayed Silvikrin hairspray to hold it in place.

This would be my first real date. I'd had a boy walk me home from a dance but had never actually been on a date. I had been working in St Teresa's children's home in Middlesbrough. Another assistant and I had gone to a Saint Patrick's Dance at the local church hall. We met two nice Irish lads there who insisted on keeping us company all night. We didn't do much dancing as I didn't know how. Afterwards they walked us back to the home. He wanted to take me out but I was leaving the following week to visit my mother in Liverpool.

'What is your favourite perfume?' he'd asked.

'I've never worn scent in my life,' I told him. He asked if I would give him my mother's address. I wondered why, as I probably wouldn't see him again.

A few days later I was in Liverpool when I received a parcel from him. Inside was a perfume called *Heaven Sent* by Helena Rubenstein. My mother was most impressed.

'It's very expensive,' she said.

I thought it more suitable for a mature woman. I gave it to my mother and she loved it.

That had been my first outing with a lad, but he'd only walked me home. This was to be my first real date.

The pub was busy when Katie and I arrived. It was standing room only at the bar.

'How are we going to find them in here?' I said to Katie, but she had already spotted them.

'There they are,' she said. 'They've saved us some seats.'

We went over to where they were sitting. I liked what I saw. He had dark curly hair, brown twinkling eyes, and a smile that lit up his face. I felt that he liked me, too.

'Hello,' he said. He turned to the lad sitting beside him. 'This is Colin and I'm Jeff.'

It was like getting the runner up prize.

'Well, I got her here, Colin,' Katie said. 'She was reluctant at first, but now she's seen you, bet she's glad she came.'

'I didn't know what to expect,' I said.

'What would you like to drink?' Jeff asked Katie and me. 'I'll have half a bitter,' Katie said.

I didn't fancy a beer. 'I'm not sure,' I said.

'I'll get you a Babycham,' Jeff replied.

I was sat on the outside next to Colin. He was sat next to Jeff and Katie was on his other side.

Jeff wanted to involve me in the conversation and had to stretch across Colin to talk to me.

'Come and sit in the middle,' he said. I ended up sitting between him and Colin.

Colin was shy at first; he didn't talk much except, maybe to ask if I wanted some crisps or another drink. The more he drank, though, the more confident he was.

He asked the usual questions. 'Where do you live?'

'I share a bedsit with Katie.'

I think he already knew that, but just said it for something to say. He asked me if I had any brothers or sisters. I didn't like to talk about my family or indeed my background. I would change the subject.

I was happy for him to talk about his family.

Colin lived with his mam and dad He talked about his two sisters, one of whom was married with a little boy. He was a Manchester City supporter. He seemed quite surprised when I showed an interest in football

I told him that I wasn't too keen on having a blind date.

'I was nervous about meeting you,' he said.

He was attentive and generous.

'Would you like another drink?' he asked as soon as I'd finished my Babycham.

He went to the bar and came back with another.

'I've asked them to put a cherry in it,' he said. 'My sister always likes a cherry in her Babycham.'

Colin went to the bar and Katie went to the loo. Jeff and I were left alone.

'You're gorgeous!' he said. 'Has anyone ever told you that?'

Yes, Faye. But I didn't tell him that. *What would he think if he knew that she had a crush on me?*

A few months back, if a man had paid me a compliment, I would have blushed to the roots and been unable to string two words together. I was self conscious then and
lacked confidence.

Since I'd come to Manchester and started fending for myself I had gained confidence and was becoming more assertive, especially with the lads.

'Are you making a pass at me?' I asked him outright. He grinned and blushed.

Later, Colin asked if he could take me to the pictures. I told him I worked in one.

'We'll just go for a drink, then,' he said.

COLIN

'Colin likes you,' Katie said when we got back to the bedsit. 'He must do, he's asked you for a date. I think he's smitten.'

'Go away, he hardly knows me.'

'Ooh, I think its love at first sight.'

Not for me it wasn't. 'Colin's a nice lad,' I said, 'but I don't fancy him.'

'Jeff said it would be great to make a foursome again.'

'Did he?'

'Wouldn't you just want to be on your own with Jeff?'

'Well yeah but... Hope he's not one of those lads who has to take his mate everywhere with him. He's suggested we go to the pictures.'

'Not where I work I hope.'

Monday was my day off. Katie and I were sat in our bedsit. We had been experimenting with the latest make up. I had panda eyes. There was a knock on the door. It was Faye. She had Colin with her. 'Found this lad waiting on the front door step,' she said.

Colin stood there looking sheepish

'These are for you,' he said and he handed me a bunch of flowers.

'Ooh, I'm jealous,' Faye said.

I'd never in my life been given a bunch of flowers. *What do I do with them? Where do I put them?* It seemed a real old fashioned thing to give to an eighteen-year-old.

103

'It's romantic,' Katie said.

We didn't have any vases so I just put them in the sink.

I was all embarrassed, the place was upside down but Colin didn't seem to mind. 'I'll leave you two alone,' Katie said. 'I'll just nip and see Faye.'

'You don't have to go,' I said, but she didn't take the hint.

Colin sat in the armchair.

I made him a cup of tea and did most of the talking. Now he was sober he wasn't as talkative as when we were in the pub. I found it hard work.

'That was nice of you, to get me the flowers,' I said.

'It was my sister's idea. She thought it would be a nice thing to do. We weren't sure what kind to get you. My mother said to get you roses, you can't go wrong.'

I hated Roses.

I remembered helping Mother Phillipa, our headmistress, plant flowers in the border and had pricked myself on thorny roses. I couldn't tell him that.

'So, you have told your family about me?' I asked.

'Oh yes, they want to meet you. That's why I've come here. They've asked me to invite you to our house for tea on Sunday.'

Oh no, that's all I need, a readymade family. I'd managed without one growing up, now I was to have one planted on me.

This was all going at too much of a fast pace. *How do I get out of it?* I was thinking of an escape plan when he stood up.

'I'd better go now,' he said. 'I'm meeting the lads. I'll come for you on Sunday about one o'clock.'

'Erm, ok,' I said reluctantly.

'Katie, how am I supposed to get out of it without hurting his feelings?' I asked after Colin had gone.

'Just go and meet his family. You can always tell him afterwards. His mam might have made special arrangements.'

How had it come to this? Now I would have to see it through. 'I'll probably be bored stiff.'

'He's just shy, that's all,' Katie said.

'And boring,' I thought.

MRS LOWE

'Well would you believe it,' Mrs Lowe said. 'I opened my door this morning and there were my candlestick. It was wrapped in an old piece of cloth. Perhaps the thief has a conscience after all.'

She was sat in Faye's bedsit, sipping tea. Katie and I were also there.

'Would you believe it?' Faye said as she looked around. 'A thief with a conscience.'

It was difficult not to laugh. We knew who had returned it. Dougie was sat in the armchair holding a cup of tea and with a smug look on his face.

'I'm really glad that they're returned it,' Mrs Lowe said, 'because I was dreading telling my son. He worries about me living on my own and wants me to sell up and move nearer to him and his family. He's heard from neighbours that the police are frequent visitors to this house.'

'That's cos we're law abiding citizens,' Faye laughed.

'I told him that my tenants are decent people. I might get the odd one that's up to no good,' she said looking at Dougie.

'Hey Mrs Lowe, I hope you're not referring to me,' Dougie said.

'Whatever made you think that?' Mrs Lowe said grinning at us.

'Anyway, I've had a more secure lock put on my door. My handyman reckons they got in too easily.'

'You're not thinking of selling the house are you?' Faye asked

'I might have to. It costs a lot to keep this place going. I may even have to put the rent up.'

'Oh don't do that Mrs Lowe,' Dougie said, 'I don't fancy living on the street.'

'Well you can always find a warm cell for the night,' she said and she winked at us.

'Ah don't be like that, Mrs. Lowe. Anytime there's a break-in the cops come looking

for me. And I haven't done nowt.'

'Why do they come here all the time looking for you?'

'They just like me company,' Dougie grinned.

'Anyway, how's Liam?' she asked. 'I haven't seen him for awhile?'

'He's made it up with that Robbie,' Faye said.

'How do you know?' I asked Faye.

'He's got a whopping black eye.

'Oh no!' I said. I was alarmed.

'He's staying with Dean, that mate of his,' Faye said.

Mrs Lowe shook her head. 'Let's hope that Robbie doesn't do any more damage to this house, or to Liam.'

THE FAMILY

'That old man actually smiled at me,' I said to Katie. 'For weeks he's just gave me a blank look when I've passed him on the stairs.'

'He's been through a lot, hasn't he?' she replied.

'I don't know much about the war,' I said, 'I wasn't born then, but that Hitler must be burning in hell now. They'll be no purgatory for him. That's where the nuns said you would go to atone for your sins but Hitler was way past redemption.'

It was Sunday afternoon and I was getting ready for Colin to call.

'I'm not looking forward to this,' I said. 'Wish I could get out of it. It's ridiculous. I've only been on one date with him and a blind one at that. Now I'm expected to meet his parents and the rest of his family. Do I need their approval?'

'He likes you a lot,' Katie said.

'So you keep saying.'

'I don't think he can believe his luck, that he's got a girl like you.'

'What do you mean, a girl like me?' I snapped. I was in a bad mood. I would have much preferred to spend the afternoon lazing around the bedsit reading my magazines. 'Well I tell you something, I'm not even interested in going out with Colin.'

'He'll be really upset if you don't go.'

'I know. That's why I can't let him down. I'd feel terrible. Ah well, I'll know the next time. When I go on a date with a lad we won't mention our families.'

There was a knock at the door. It was Colin.

'You're early,' Katie said. 'You must be keen.' Colin blushed.

'Better early than late,' he said.

We walked to the bus stop. 'It's a Sunday service,' he said, the buses only run every hour. We're going to arrive early at me mam's, but she won't mind.'

That's just great, I thought.

The bus took us to a district of a Manchester called Longsight. We arrived at a terraced house.

'Do you think we should arrive so early?' I asked. After all, I thought, I wouldn't like anyone calling if I wasn't ready for them. I was getting butterflies in my stomach. I didn't know why, because I certainly had no intentions of marrying him.

He opened the door. I took a deep breath and followed him inside. We went into the living room. 'Mam, she's here,' he shouted.

His mother was in the kitchen. She came out wiping her hands on her apron.

'You're early, our Colin,' she said.

'This is Anne.'

'Nice to meet you. He's never shut up talking about you. Sit down, chucks, I'll make you a cuppa.'

We sat down on the three seater settee.

She went into the kitchen. I looked around the living room. The walls were adorned with photographs of babies and children at various stages in their lives. There was a photo of a baby with chubby pink cheeks.

'I bet that's you,' I said.

'Yeah, how did you guess?

'I recognised your smile,' I said. He grinned. The baby was wearing a blue romper suit. He had told me that his other siblings were girls.

'Where's the rest of the family?'

'Me dad's down at the pub, but he'll be back at closing time. Me sister will be here soon. She'll be bringing our Ollie with her.'

His mother came into the room. She was carrying a tray with three mugs of tea on it.

'We've an hour to go til the trifles set she said. We'll make do with a cuppa for now. Colin says you're not from round here.'

'No, I'm from Middlesbrough.'

'Where's that? I've never heard of it.'

'It's in the North East.'

'Do your parents mind you living away from home?'

'Not really.'

What would she think if I'd told her the truth, that I'd lived away from home all my life?

The front door was slung open and a little boy came running into the room.

'Ah, how's my little angel?' Colin's mother said as she grabbed him and gave him a hug.

'Uncle Colin, I got a new aeroplane,' the child said. He opened his chubby fingers. It was a tiny replica of a spitfire. He went zooming round the room.

A young woman peeked her head round the door.

'Hi,' she said. 'So you've arrived? Just have to nip to the loo, mam. I'm dying for a pee.'

'What's she like?' Colin's mam said, looking slightly embarrassed.

I liked his family. And when his dad came back from the pub and was introduced to me I liked them even more.

'Bloody heck, our Colin, I wish I were twenty years younger,' he said as he shook hands with me.

We passed a pleasant afternoon. I was full up after the roast dinner and the trifle dessert. His dad kept cracking jokes. I told him I liked George Best.

'What, that poofter! He should get his hair cut.'

'What, with all those girl friends he has,' his wife said.

'Dad doesn't like him cos he's a Manchester United player, and we're City supporters through and through,' Colin explained.

Colin walked me to the bus stop.

'You don't have to take me all the way home,' I said.

'His family's really down to earth,' I said to Katie when I got back. 'His dad's a scream. It was real funny when he fell asleep in the chair and was snoring his head off. I think his mam was embarrassed but it didn't bother me at all.'

LIAM AND ROBBIE

'**W**hy does Liam put up with that Robbie,' I said, 'when he's always beating him up?'

Faye shook her head. 'Probably cos he loves him,' she said.

'How can you love someone who's always hitting you and giving you black eyes? I don't understand it.'

In Nazareth House you may have got a thrashing from the nuns or the senior girls. But, you had no choice but to put up with it, or hide as I once did when Mother Superior was out to get me. But to go back time and time again for more of the same was beyond me. I was annoyed and frustrated with Liam.

'I wish that Robbie was back in the nick,' I'd say.

A few days earlier we had all been laughing and giggling as we watched Dean and Liam come down the stairs dressed as Judy Garland and Marilyn Monroe. They were taking part in a drag contest at the club. Dean's high heel had got caught on the step and he was complaining about having a ladder in his nylons. He lifted his skirt up just as Dougie came out of his bedsit. Dougie whistled appreciatory. 'That's a nice leg. Now if I didn't know that you were a fella I might ask you out.'

'You couldn't afford us, Dougie,' Liam said. 'We're high maintenance.'

Tanya got her nail varnish and applied it to Dean's nylons.

'That should stop the run,' she said.

I asked if they were getting a taxi. 'You're not going down the street dressed like that?'

It was still illegal to be gay in 1966. And I'd heard some horror stories of guys being beaten up. I was relieved when they said that a friend was picking them up in his car. We'd waved them off with cheerful banter.

Now, a few days later, here was Liam wearing dark glasses, his face bruised and more subdued than the last time I'd seen him.

Apparently, Dean and Liam had gone to the club and had a great time but afterwards Liam wanted to avoid Robbie who was waiting outside. Dean and Liam had sneaked out the back door. They had gone to a party at a friend's house and had stayed there for a few days until Robbie had found him.

'I hope that someone gives *him* a black eye,' I said to Faye. 'Does his wife know about Liam?'

'Probably not. He ain't exactly going to say to her that is he messing around with a fella. Can you imagine the conversation? I suspect he won't be telling her anything. He most likely beats her up as well.'

'What a nasty piece.'

'He's quite nice when you get to know him,' Faye said. 'Anytime I see him out he always buys me and Jo a drink.'

'And you call that being nice?'

'Well you can have a decent conversation with him when he's sober. He seems to know a lot. He's not daft.'

'No, Liam's the one who's daft,' I said.

'You can't run people's lives for 'em,' Faye said. 'Liam's not a kid. It's when Robbie's had too much to drink he goes crazy.'

'Well then he shouldn't drink at all,' I said.

'I wouldn't like to be the barman who tried to stop him. He would probably smash the place up.'

'That man's a maniac,' I said to Katie when we were back in our bedsit.

'Do you think that he's mad at Liam for turning him queer? Is that why he beats him up?' I said.

'Don't be daft. Queers are born that way, not made.'

'Who told you that?

'Faye and she should know. She said that he may have fancied men but when his girlfriend got pregnant he had to marry her.'

'Had to! I can't see him being forced into doing anything.'

'Anyway he's got more kids now, about three I think. Faye told me.'

'He's a sex maniac,' Katie and I agreed.

MADAME JOSEPHINA

It was a Saturday afternoon and Katie and I were in our bedsit when I heard a knock at the front door. Rita had gone out to the shops but I had given her a key to the front door. 'It won't be her knocking,' I thought. As usual none of other tenants in the house were in a hurry to answer it. Although Dougie had a bedsit on the ground floor he tended to ignore the sound of knocking. "It might be the cops," he would say.

Our bedsit overlooked the front of the house. I peered out of the window and saw a smartly dressed man standing on the doorstep. He knocked on the door again. Katie looked up from reading a magazine. "Who is it?" she asked.

"I don't know," I replied. "He looks like a salesman. He could be selling something."

Katie laughed. "What! Selling something here? He's wasting his time, there's nobody in this house got two halfpennies to rub together."

"If he doesn't stop knocking on the door," I said, "it'll wake Scots Billy and he'll be in a bad mood."

"He'll probably tell him to F... off," Katie replied. Both Dougie and Scots Billy were night owls. They stayed out until the early hours of the morning and slept most of the day. Often we would not see them until later in the evening.

The knocking was persistent. "I'd better go and see what he wants," I said.

I ran down the stairs and opened the front door. Stood on the doorstep was a middle aged man with silver graying hair. He looked quite distinguished.

"Good afternoon," he said. "I am sorry to bother you but I have come to see Madam Josephina."

"I beg your pardon?" I replied, not sure if I had heard correctly.

"Please could you tell Madam Josephina that I would like to see her?"

I was puzzled. "Madam Josephina? I'm sorry, there is no one with that name living here."

"Oh but there is," he said.

I was getting concerned. I didn't want to let this strange man into the house. I didn't know if he was a nutcase or what, but he was ever so polite.

"I will just make some enquiries," I replied.

"Thank you," he said.

"Please do not knock again as there are people sleeping, but I will have to close the door."

"That is alright. I understand. I will wait while you inform Madam Josephina that I am here."

I went up the stairs. Madam Josephina? I wondered if he was looking for a fortune teller. I knocked on Faye's door. It was a while before she answered.

"Who is it?" she asked.

"It's me, Anne," I told her. She opened the door dressed in her pyjamas. She had just woken up and the curtains were still drawn in her room. She had obviously had a late night. She blinked in the light and rubbed the sleep from her eyes.

"Oh you're a sight for sore eyes," she said. "Have you come to see me?"

"Behave yourself Faye! Sorry to have woken you but there's a strange man at the front door. He's asking for a Madam Josephina? Do you know anyone with that name? He's adamant she lives here."

"What's he look like?" she asks.

"He's middle aged and looks dead posh," I replied.

"Bloody 'ell," she said and went back into the bedsit. She mumbled something to Jo who came out of the bedroom holding a cigarette delicately between two fingers.

She had rollers in her hair under a chiffon scarf and was wearing a pastel blue nylon night gown which left nothing to the imagination. She winked at me as she passed and went scurrying down the stairs, flinging open the front door and before the man had a chance to open his mouth she threw a tirade of abuse at him. She was very angry.

"How dare you come to my door?" she shouted. "How dare you disobey me? You will be severely punished for this."

I am horrified. 'How rude of Jo,' I thought, 'and how strange for her to speak in such an authoritative way, so unlike her.'

Faye was grinning and puffing hard on a cigarette. She noticed how horrified I was.

"Don't fret," she said. "He's lapping it up. He's one of her clients. He's the kinky one." She laughed. "Oh, I wouldn't want to get on the wrong side of Madam Josephina." Then it clicked.

"I have just about heard it all now," I said to Katie after I got back to our bedsit and related what had happened.

"Maybe you could get him to clean your boots," she replied.

We did tease Jo for days afterwards. "Would Madam Josephina like us to get her some cigarettes from the shop?" we would ask. She would grin and then say, "Bugger off and stop taking the piss."

El DORADO

It was Tania's twentieth birthday and a good excuse for a party. She had invited us into her room for celebratory drinks before she went out to see to business.

'Don't you even have a night off for your birthday?' Katie asked her.

'It's the best time. When I tell my punters that it's me birthday, they'll give me some extra dough.'

Dougie was there with his girlfriend. They were only popping in for the one as she would be working in the club later on. There were already bottles of various drinks on the table. Tania had set out some mugs. Katie and I sat on the bed. The door was open and Scots Billy walked in carrying bottles of wine. He opened the bottles, filled our mugs almost to the brim and handed them to Katie and me. 'Here hen,' he said to Katie, 'have a taste of this.'

'What's this?' I asked.

'It's called El Dorado and I brought it all the way from bonnie Scotland,' he said.

It tasted quite sweet. I much preferred it to beer.

'Yeah, I like it,' I said.

'So, you managed to find that thieving swine who nicked Mrs Lowe's candelabra?' Tania said. 'Mrs Lowe was over the moon to get it back.'

'Aye, I did,' Scots Billy said, 'and I give him a good hiding. He'll no steal from me in a hurry.'

'He shit himself when he saw us,' Dougie said. 'He tried to make a run for it, but he didn't get far.'

119

'Did you get your stuff back?'

'No, the bastard's sold the lot.'

Scots Billy took out a tin of tobacco and rolled himself a cigarette.

'We've just passed that old man on the stairs. He's coming out of his shell. He's tried to make conversation with me but I couldn't understand a word he was saying. He's a foreigner. Mind you, half the time I barely understand Billy,' Dougie grinned.

'Cheeky bastard, it's you Sassenachs who canna speak properly.'

'Which part of Scotland are you from?' I asked Billy.

'Glasgow.'

'My mother's from there,' I said.

'Which part of Glasgow is she from?'

'I don't know,' I said.

'Are you any relatives still up there? Fancy going up to see 'em?'

'I wouldn't know where to look.'

'Your ma never kept in touch with 'em?'

She hardly kept in touch with me and my sister, but I didn't want to tell him that.

'I d like to see the Lochness Monster,' I said.

'Ooh, so would I,' Katie said. 'Do you know, I think there's bit of Irish in me.'

'We've all got some foreign blood in us,' Dougie said.

'Hey, you speak for yerself,' Tania said. 'I'm Lancashire through and through.' She had a cigarette in one hand and a drink in the other and she was getting quite tipsy.

She burst into song.

She's a lassie from Lancashire,
Just a lassie from Lancashire,
She's the lassie that I love dear,
Oh! So dear.
Though she dresses in clogs and shawl,
She's the prettiest of them all.
As none can be fairer or rarer than Sarah,
My lassie from Lancashire.

'Me granddad used to sing it to me granny,' she said.

Katie and I gave her a round of applause.

More wine was poured into our mugs. I drank it quickly. Apart from feeling quite warm it didn't seem to have an effect on me at all, or so I thought.

Billy turned to Katie and me. 'How's that lassie that's up the stick? Are you still putting her up?'

'Yes,' Katie said, 'she's nowhere else to go. It's a squash in our bedsit. And we have to keep telling Mrs Lowe that she's just visiting. She'll cotton on one of these days.'

'She could stay in my place for a wee while,' he said. I'm going back up the road. The polis 'll be looking for me soon, if that bastard reports me. Woudna put it past him. I've heard he's a grass.'

'That would be great,' Katie and I agreed. I was fed up of sleeping in the armchair.

'How soon are you thinking of going?' I asked.

'There's an overnight bus leaves Piccadilly the night. I'll be on it.'

121

Tania was looking at her birthday cards. There was one from Faye and Jo, Katie and me and Liam.

One of the birthday cards read *To a Dear Daughter*.

'That's from me mam,' Tania said. 'I'll have to pop round and see her one of these days.'

'Do you not see much of her then?' I asked.

'No, and it's better that way. We only argue. That's the reason I left home in the first place. We were always at each other's throats.'

'Does she know what you do for a living?' Dougie grinned.

'Bloody 'ell no. She'd go mad.'

'She must think a lot of you, though, for her to send you such a nice birthday card,' I said. I remembered receiving a similar card from my mother when I was in the orphanage. I had been delighted as with Mother it was hit and miss whether you got one or not. The birthday card had pink scented flowers on it. I treasured it for days and proudly showed it to the other girls.

Tania picked up the birthday card, opened it and took her time to read the verse. When she put it down again, there were tears in her eyes.

'Where are Faye and Jo?' Dougie asked. 'It's not like them to miss up on a free drink.'

'They've gone to the pictures to see *Zorba the Greek*,' I said. 'I got the tickets for them. This wine certainly warms you up. I'll have another glass.'

Billy filled the mug up to the brim and did the same for Katie.

'So, you fancy seeing the Lochness Monster?' he asked.

'Oooh yeah,' Katie and I said.

'Well, I'm going to Scotland tonight. Come with us.'

'Yes, let's go,' I said. It was the drink talking. Next thing I remember is Katie and I in a taxi, heading for Piccadilly bus station.

Apparently, we couldn't get on the same bus as Scots Billy. There was no room so we'd jumped on another bus.

When I sobered up I was travelling on a bus. I had no recollection of how we'd ended up there. Katie was by my side and she was fast asleep. We had no coats on and it was freezing cold. I was wearing my slippers. We told the driver we wanted to go back to Manchester. He let us get off the bus at Newcastle bus terminus.

'Why were you going to Glasgow?' the driver inquired.

'We wanted to see the Lochness Monster,' Katie said.

'That was a wasted journey,' he said. 'You'll no find her there, hen. She's alive and well and living next door ta me.'

We giggled so much my head hurt.

We had to hang around the bus station until we could catch another bus back to Manchester. I had one gigantic hangover and Katie was sick. I had the worst headache ever.

I don't know what was in the drink, but it was pretty potent stuff.

BABY PREPARATIONS

'It's OK for now,' Mrs Lowe said. 'Rita can stay in Scots Billy's bedsit, as long as the rent is paid.'

Rita was delighted. Katie and I helped her clean the bedsit before she moved in. I helped her take the bedding to the laundrette. Katie said it couldn't have worked out better.

'I'll have to go home and get my clothes,' she said, 'but I'm scared in case me dad's there.'

'We'll come with you,' Katie and I said. 'He won't hit you in front of us. Or better still, we can send Faye round, she'll sort him out.'

'Ooh no,' Rita laughed. 'I can imagine me dad's face if Faye turned up. He'll think I've gone queer.'

Rita was now eight months pregnant and it was only since staying with Katie and me that she had bought a few things for the baby.

Jo was a voracious knitter. We were surprised how quickly she knitted matinee coats, booties and mittens in colours of lemon and white. Faye had a go at knitting and we laughed at her attempts as she kept dropping stitches and had to start all over again.

'I'll get the hang of it in time,' she'd say.

Dougie teased her

'We can't wait eighteen months, it's not a baby elephant she's having. It's almost due.'

'Ooh, yer cheeky bugger,' Faye said

'I'll have to contact me mam to arrange a time when me dad's not in,' Rita said.

'You'll have to order a taxi an' all,' Katie said. 'You've no transport.'

Rita was meeting her mam in the village later that afternoon to tell her she'd been offered a bedsit.

'I hope her mam doesn't go on at her about having the baby adopted,' I said.

I hadn't told Rita what her mam had said about me encouraging her to have the baby adopted. Rita was planning on keeping the baby. I didn't want to upset her.

'Perhaps she'll come round now that Rita's got somewhere to stay,' I said. I was trying to be optimistic that things would turn out OK.

'Yes, but she will still never be able to go home,' Katie said.

'So what? She can stand on her own two feet now.'

'What do you think she's gonna call the baby?' Tania asked. We were sat in Faye and Jo's bedsit drinking cups of tea.

'Well, I think she should name it Jo,' Tania said, 'after all those baby clothes she's knitted for it. Joseph if it's boy, and maybe Josephine if it's a girl.'

'That makes sense,' Faye said. 'It'll end up being shortened to Jo.'

Jo came in carrying the knitted baby clothes. She placed them on her lap then lifted one item up at a time to show us.

'Aw, isn't that cute, isn't that tiny?' we commented as each item was shown.

'This is Faye's contribution,' Jo said and held up a pair of misshapen baby mittens.

Faye grinned. 'I can't read a bloody knitting pattern. Thought it said knit a stitch drop a stitch.'

'Never mind, Faye, it's the thought that counts,' we said.

Rita came back from the village. She'd been crying.

'Me mam says I'd better not go home, and that she'll bring me clothes to me. She's worried what the neighbours might think.'

'Bloody 'ell,' Faye said. 'She's worried about what the neighbours might think?'

Rita nodded. 'I came in with that old man that has the bedsit upstairs. He was staring at me cos I was that upset. I bet he was wondering what was wrong with me. He said summit to me in a foreign language.'

A few days later, I went downstairs to Rita's bedsit to take her some baby clothes. I was about to knock on her door when I heard voices being raised. There was an argument going on.

I stood outside the door and listened.

'You can't bring a new baby back here. It's a doss house. How are you going to manage?'

I recognised the voice of Rita's mother.

'You can't live here amongst the riffraff,' another woman was saying. 'Listen to yer mam. We've only got your interests at heart.'

Yes, I bet you have. If you had her interests at heart she wouldn't be living here in the first place, I thought.

'I'm not having the baby adopted,' Rita shouted. 'You can't make me. I don't care what my dad or the neighbours say.'

Why are they upsetting her at this late stage in her pregnancy? I was annoyed.

126

I knocked on the door. 'Is Rita there?' I asked.

It was opened by a woman I hadn't seen before. 'Who are you?' she said.

'I live upstairs,' I said. I was tempted to add, 'I'm one of the riffraff.'

Rita came to the door. She'd been crying. Her eyes were red.

'Are you alright?' I said. She nodded.

'I see you've got company.'

'It's me mam and me Aunty Jane,' she said.

'I'll call back later,' I said.

'They were putting pressure on her to have the baby adopted,' I said to Katie. 'And do you know what that aunty of hers called this place? A doss house.'

'Don't let Mrs Lowe hear you saying that,' said Katie. 'Even if it is true.'

JEFF

'There's a handsome young man asking for you,' Norma said.

'Who, me?'

'Yes you,' she said. 'He's in the foyer.'

It was Jeff. 'What are you doing here?' I asked.

'I've come to see you. What time do you finish?' he asked.

'I'm still on duty. I won't be able to talk for long.'

'Well can I take you out on when you're free?'

'You're supposed to be seeing Katie. She'll be really disappointed if she thinks you are two timing her.'

'I'll tell her it's over. I don't want to see her anymore.'

'You can't do that.'

'Why not, it's not that I've been going out with her for long. She'll get over it.'

'Katie likes you a lot you know. She's even made plans for your birthday. And what about Colin, he's your best friend?'

'He'll understand. He'll be ok about it.'

'I'm not so sure. He's asked me to be his fiancée. He wants to buy me an engagement ring.'

'I know, he's told me. That's why I want to see you before it's too late.'

'I have no intention of getting engaged to Colin or to anyone,' I said. 'I was stunned when he asked me. It's all going too fast for me. It's ridiculous, I hardly know him. Was he like that with other girls?'

128

'No, never.'

Out of the corner I could see Ethel anxiously looking our way. The picture was about to end and I would be needed to supervise the patrons out of the door.

'I'll have to go now,' I said.

'Can I meet you later?'

'I don't know.'

'What time do you finish work?'

'Half past ten.'

'I'll come and meet you then,' he said and before I had time to change my mind he was out of the door.

'Is that the boyfriend?' Ethel asked.

'No, but he would like to be.'

'Why not?' she said. 'He's a good looking boy.

'It's not as simple as that. He belongs to someone else. She thinks the world of him an' all.'

'Eeh, there're more drama off the screen in this place than there is on it,' she grinned.

Jeff was waiting for me when I came out of the door. Norma and the other staff smiled at us. They obviously thought we were a couple. 'Let's go for a drink,' Jeff said.

'I need to get back to the bedsit,' I said. 'I can't miss my bus.'

'Don't worry, I'll pay for a taxi for you,' he said.

There was a pub nearby. There weren't many customers in the lounge. We sat down at a small round table.

He went to the bar and came back with a pint for him and a Babycham for me. 'I've made sure they put the cherry on it,' he said.

It felt strange just the two of us sat there, without Katie or Colin.

If only Katie and Colin could get together, that would be the ideal solution.

'I should have come out that night Katie met you. She asked me, you know, but I was working. I suppose I could have changed shifts with one of the other girls.'

Colin had asked me out again. We had made a foursome with his sister and her husband. It had been a good night. I was finding out that if we were in company it was fun but when I was with Colin alone I was bored. We didn't have anything in common. He had his good points and was very family orientated. He adored his little nephew and talked endlessly about the things he got up to and how cheeky he was. 'I can't wait to have kids of my own,' he said. I could see my life stretched out ahead of me if I were to marry him. It would have been a life of kids and grudge. I'd had all that growing up with nuns. I wanted more. I wanted excitement. I wanted to explore the world and this life that I had been isolated from for all these years. I wanted to be one of the 'outside girls' for a change.

Jeff was a Manchester United supporter. They were on to a winning streak. The newspapers were full of the antics of Georgie Best and his girlfriend.

'He's a fantastic player,' Jeff said. 'You want to see him in action when he gets the ball. You always expect him to score a goal.'

'I'd like to see him reduce the cost of those clothes in his boutique,' I said.

130

We finished our drinks and ambled our way to the taxi stand. My head was fuzzy and filled with mixed emotions. *How do I tell Katie that Jeff and I fancy each other? And what about Colin?* I should have not let it get this far. *What would his family think of me?* They had accepted me with open arms. I could easily have been swept along and become part of my first real family but I knew that I would have been living a lie.

The taxi came. Jeff turned to kiss me but I hopped into the taxi. I didn't want to be deceitful, but that was easier said than done.

FALLOUT

I open the front door and I'm surprised to see Faye standing at the bottom of the stairs surrounded by an assortment of clothes. Jo is at the top of the stairs throwing more clothes down. She's very angry.
Dougie and Rita are standing there just watching it all. There's a bemused look on their faces.

'I won't be put out of my home for you or anyone,' Jo shouts.

Faye is trying to remonstrate with her. 'Aw, don't be like that, Jo,' she says.

'What's that all about?' I ask Rita.

'Faye and Jo have had a fallout,' she says.

'Why?'

'Faye's sister is coming round at the weekend. She's bringing Faye's son and she wants Jo to keep out of the way while they're here.'

'That's a bit harsh,' I say.

'I will not be thrown out of my own home,' Jo is shouting, 'for you, her or anybody.

'If you are ashamed of me then *you* can go.'

'There's plenty more fish in the sea,' Jo is shouting. 'I do not need you, my dear. I have come down in the world since I met you.'

'It's only for a day, Jo,' Faye pleads. 'I'll make it up to you, Jo.'

Tania comes out of her bedsit. She's heard them arguing.

'You can use my bedsit, Faye,' she shouts down the stairs, 'if you want somewhere to bring the lad. I'll be away at the weekend.'

'Nice of you to offer,' Faye says as she ducks to avoid shoes and coats being flung down on top of her.

'Careful, Jo! You'll bash me brains in!'

'What brains? If you had any you'd tell that weirdo family of yours where to go.'

'But he wants to stay overnight, Jo, and see where I live.'

'He can stay as far as I'm concerned but I have no intention of hiding from him.'

'You'll just have to face it then, Faye,' Dougie says. 'Fuck 'em, it's your life.'

'You don't know what my family's like. I have to keep things normal for the lad.'

'What's normal about living in this house?' Dougie grins

'It's only for one night,' Faye says.

'If you don't go,' Jo shouts, 'then I will. And if I do, I won't be coming back.' She goes back into her bedsit slamming the door shut behind her.

'Come in me bedsit, Faye,' Dougie says, 'til Jo's calmed down. You and Rita come in as well. You can have a cup of char as long as Rita makes it.'

'What a bloody cheek,' Rita says.

But she amiably goes over to the stove and puts the kettle on.

Dougie's bedsit is at the back of the house and looks out onto the overgrown back garden.

He is a prolific cigarette smoker and the ash tray is overflowing.

'Do you ever do any washing up?' Rita asks as she takes some mugs out of the sink.

'No, I leave that to you,' he says. 'You do such a good job.'

Since moving into Scots Billy's bedsit Rita often pops in to see Dougie. They get on like a house on fire.

'Just tell him you're good friends and that you share a bedsit,' Rita advises Faye. 'Anne and Katie share a bedsit and they're just friends.'

'Can you not just tell him the truth?' Dougie says

'Ooh no, I couldn't. When the old bird was pissed she was arguing with our Iris about me. The lad overheard them talking about us. He got all upset and said 'me mam's not a queer'. So that's what I'm up against.'

'He's gonna have to know sooner or later,' I say.

'Yeah, but he'll be old enough to understand then,' she says.

'But wouldn't it be better to tell him now so he can get used to it,' Rita suggests. 'If you wait too long it might come as such a shock to him. What if he wants to come and live with you?' she asks.

'Nah, he's happy living with me mam. She's brought him up. I saw a lot of him when I lived in Blackpool. Not so much these days since moving here. Me mam blames Jo. Said I'd be living back at home if it weren't for her. But that's not true.'

'Couldn't he live with you and Jo?' I ask.

'He'd have a rotten time at school if they found out he were living with a couple of lesbos.'

There's a knock on the door. It's Tania. 'I mean it, Faye,' she says, 'you can use my bedsit. I don't like to see you and Jo fall out. Maybe you should postpone it 'til she gets used to the idea.'

'Can't do that. I'm taking him to the Man United match. It's a treat for his birthday. I can't let him down. Jo's being selfish,' Faye says.

'Maybe she thinks it's time you told him the truth about you and Jo,' Rita says. 'It would be good to get it of your chest. I feel so much better now me family knows about the baby. For months I were worried about how they would react when I told them. I know I didn't get the response I would have liked but at least now it's out in the open it's a load of me mind.'

True to her word, Jo walked out taking all her things with her. Faye was out on the town at the time. We heard Dougie shouting up the stairs, 'Jo, there's a taxi waiting for you.'

Katie and I came out of our bedsit. We'd heard Jo threatening to leave Faye but didn't think that she'd go through with it. Now here she was coming down the stairs carrying a case.

'Where will you stay, Jo?' Dougie asked as he took the case from her. 'You know Faye will be lost without ya.'

Katie and I tried to get her to stay.

'We can sort something out, Jo,' I said.

'Ah don't go, Jo,' Katie pleaded.

'She's not going to treat me like that every time any of her relations come here. She can choose between them or me.'

'But where will you go?'

135

She looked at our anxious faces. 'Don't worry about me. I'm staying with a cousin for a few days. Look after Faye will you.' She took her case from Dougie and went out the front door, closing it behind her.

'I don't wanna be around when Faye gets back,' Dougie said. 'She'll go fucking mad.'

'What do you think she'll do, Dougie?' I asked.

'She'll be pissed. I wouldn't be surprised if she wrecks the place.'

'She wouldn't do a Robbie would she?'

Dougie laughed, 'Well yer know what they say about a woman scorned.'

'It's no laughing matter, Dougie,' Katie said.

'I know it isn't but I feel for Jo. I'm surprised that Faye couldn't tell that family of hers to fuck off.'

'But there's a bairn involved,' Katie said.

Dougie shrugged his shoulders. 'I'm off for a pint,' he said.

Later, Katie and I lay in our beds. We were on tenterhooks, waiting for Faye to return.

'What would you have done, Katie, if you were in Faye's situation?' I asked.

'Dunno, why?'

'I would wait for the lad to ask me and then I'd tell him the truth.'

'But then he'd have to keep it secret from everyone, even his mates at school. It's not something you can brag about.'

'I think I understand,' I said. I certainly knew what it was like to be an outcast.

I dropped off to sleep. I was awoken in the early hours of the morning by a large crashing sound. Katie stirred. We heard raised voices. I jumped out of bed.

'Faye's home,' I whispered to Katie.

'Do you think we should just leave her to sober up?' she asked.

Faye was shouting at the top of her voice. 'She's fucking left me, Dougie. She's took all her stuff. Look, the wardrobe's empty.' We hear the door being flung back against the wall.

Dougie is trying to calm her down. 'Faye, she's only gone for few days so your lad can stay.'

'No, she's fucking gone for good,' Faye said.

'I think we should go and see her,' I said. 'We're not going to get much sleep now.'

The door to Faye's bedsit was wide open. Katie and I went into the room. Faye was slouched in the armchair, a glass of whisky in one hand and a cigarette in the other.

'Jo's left me,' she said as she puffed hard on a cigarette.

'No, she hasn't. I've told you, she's keeping out of the way until the lad's been. She told us, didn't she?' Dougie said and he looked at Katie and me.

I was lost for words. I didn't know what to say.

Katie and I sat on the ottoman and listened until Faye's ranting had subsided and she'd fallen asleep. We tiptoed back to our bedsit leaving Dougie lying on the bed and snoring loudly.

Now Faye was on her own the bedsit was in a mess. Faye hit the bottle. She went round to Jo's cousin's house on a posh estate and put a brick through the

137

window. Jo didn't press charges. We went into her room and it was a mess. Ash trays were overflowing and the sink full of dirty crockery.

'Even my place is cleaner than this,' Dougie joked.

It wasn't only Faye who missed Jo, we did too. She was the motherly one who made us cups of tea and gave advice. A few weeks later Katie and I bumped into Jo in the town. We told her that Faye was drinking herself into oblivion. 'We're concerned about her,' we said. Jo seemed worried. 'Dougie says she'll end up in the nick, the way she gets sozzled. He said you need to talk to her.'

Faye was proud. 'I wouldn't have her back if she begged me,' she said. Tania, Dougie, Katie and I were in her room. We tried to tidy up. We washed the crockery. Even Rita did her best to help. 'Send her flowers,' she suggested.

After all the fuss it had caused it was Faye's sister who had taken Karl to the football match and had taken him back home afterwards. I did feel for the lad though as he had missed the opportunity of spending some time with his mam. And I know just how precious those moments can be.

A week later and Katie and I were in our beds. It was nearly midnight. We heard loud singing from outside. Katie jumped out of bed and made her way to the window.

'Come and see this,' she said. I joined her at the window. Faye and the old man were coming up the path. They were doing the dance from *Zorba the Greek*. The front door was flung open and we heard

138

footsteps coming up the stairs. They stopped at Faye's bedsit.

Katie and I wondered who it could be. Faye and the old man were singing as they came in the front door.

'Alright, Anthony Quinn, get your arse up here and open the door. I can't find my key.'

'Yes, Jo, whatever you say, darlin'.'

Katie and I giggled.

'Oh, I'm so glad they're back together,' I said

'Me too,' Katie said. 'We'll get a decent night's sleep now.'

A CHILD IS BORN

Katie and I were at work when Rita went into labour. She was a few weeks from her due date and was complaining of stomach pains. Katie and I tried to persuade her to go to the hospital.

'It's just indigestion,' she said.

Faye and Jo had gone downstairs to check on her. Dougie said that he would keep an eye on her too.

Later that morning Dougie had come banging on Faye's door.

She told us what had happened.

'I thought he were being chased by the cops the way he come running up them stairs. He were as white as a sheet. You'd have thought he were the dad. 'I think she's having the baby,' he said.

'I sent him next door to Mrs Lowe's to phone for a taxi.

'Then I had to tell the taxi driver to get a move on. 'She could have the baby any minute,' I said. Well, you should have seen him go, he were faster than Stirling Moss on a race track. Jo were sat in the back seat keeping Rita calm and I'm in front with the driver. He kept looking behind. He were terrified Rita were gonna have the baby in the car.

'When we got to the hospital the nurse wouldn't let us stay with her. They shaved her and gave her an enema and after all that it was a false alarm. But they kept her in as her blood pressure was high.

'Rita didn't want to tell her mam 'til she'd had the baby, but me and Jo were worried. I mean what if owt happens to her? We don't know her medical background.'

The decision was taken out of their hands, though, when Rita's aunty had called round to the bedsit and Dougie told her that she was in the hospital.

Faye continued, 'Rita's aunty and mam eventually turned up at the hospital. Rita were pleased to see them. They weren't so happy though, as they had to wait outside. There were too many visitors round her bedside, the nurse said.'

'I'm going to stay with me aunty,' Rita said when Katie and I went to see her. 'I don't know much about babies, but she's gonna help me with 'im.'

'I hope they don't go on at her about getting the baby adopted,' I said to Katie afterwards.

Jo was thrilled that the baby had left the hospital wearing the matinee coat and hat that she had knitted for him.

The next day Rita's mam turned up at the bedsit for Rita's things and the baby clothes. Mrs Lowe informed us that Rita wasn't coming back. Her mother settled up what she owed of the rent money.

I felt sad. We were going to miss Rita, but hoped that things would turn out all right for her. I never saw her again.

THE OLD MAN

I was awoken by a blood curdling scream. It set my heart racing. Katie and I had been in our beds sleeping. It woke us up.

'What the bloody hell is that?' Katie said. I got out of bed and listened at the door.

There it was again, another scream.

'It's coming from the floor above us,' I said. 'Oh my God, what's going on?'

'It's probably the old man,' Katie said. Faye had told us that he often had nightmares and sometimes screamed out in the night.

I heard Faye's door opening. I put my dressing gown and slippers on and unlocked our door. Faye was stood at the bottom of the stairs that led to the upper floor.

'He's having one of his nightmares,' she said. Jo came out of the room. She had rollers in her hair. Screaming and banging could be heard.

'Poor man,' she said.

'Will he be alright?' I asked. I was concerned.

'I hope so,' she said.

'Should we wake him up?' Katie asked as she joined us on the stairs.

'Ooh no,' Faye said. 'Mrs Lowe told us not to, it could scare him to death.'

'Liam must be out,' Jo said. 'He couldn't sleep through that.'

Tania came out of her bedsit just as another scream reverberated through the house. It made me shiver.

She put a cigarette in her mouth, lit it and then handed the packet around.

'I need summit to steady me nerves,' she said. 'That screaming puts me on edge.'

'He'll settle down eventually,' Faye said as she plonked herself down on one of the steps.

Katie yawned. 'How long will that take?'

'Dunno,' Faye frowned as she lit a cigarette. 'We just have to make sure he stays in his room. He could harm himself. He won't know what he's doing.'

Jo went into her bedsit and came out carrying a chair. She put it on the landing, sat down and crossed her legs.

'Do you do this often?' I asked.

'We'll have to watch out for him,' she said, as she held a cigarette between two fingers.

Tania went further up the stairs and sat on a step. I did the same.

'I may as well join you,' Katie said wearily as she sat on the bottom step. 'We won't get much sleep tonight.'

We heard a door opening downstairs and footsteps came plodding up the stairs.

'For fuck's sake,' Dougie said. 'I thought someone was being murdered. That old geezer's tormented by his past, you gotta feel sorry for him. Has anyone got a ciggie?' he asked. 'I'm desperate for a fag.'

'Liam's not here,' Faye said, as Tania handed him a cigarette.

Dougie grinned. 'Ooh, yer cheeky bugger,' he said.

More shouting was heard. It was followed by prolonged screaming. It made me shiver.

Tania jumped up.

'Jesus,' she said. 'That's bloody awful.'

'He's shouting summit in a foreign language,' Faye said.

'He must have really suffered in the war,' Tania said as she sat down again.

'He did, and he lost all his family, kids an' all,' Jo said.

'That bloody Hitler,' Faye spat as she flicked ash from her cigarette. 'Albert Pierrepoint said he'd have gladly put the noose round that Hitler's neck like he did his henchmen.'

'Albert Pierrepoint, who's he?' I asked.

'He's a hangman. I've been in the pub he used to run in Hollinwood.'

'Do you know him?' I asked.

'Yeah, me and Jo had a drink in his pub.'

'Honestly?'

'Yeah, he's very approachable and he's just doing a job. He's got a lot of respect. He's a nice man.'

'Bet those who he hung wouldn't think he was nice,' I said.

Dougie screwed his face up. 'You know some weird people Faye,' he said.

'I know, I'm looking at one now,' she said, then turned and winked at us.

'I'm going to put the kettle on,' Jo said. 'Anyone want a cuppa?'

'Ooh yeah, I'll come and help you,' Tania said, just as another scream could be heard.

'Did you hear that, Jo, your girlfriend's calling me weird?' Dougie said.

'Well it takes one to know one,' Jo laughed.

It seemed surreal sitting on the stairs in our night clothes, exchanging banter, smoking and drinking tea in the early hours of the morning while listening out for the screams of an anguished old man.

I was frightened in case he came out of his room. 'What will you do if he starts wandering about?' I asked.

'If we had to, we'd get Mrs Lowe,' Faye said. 'But we'll only do that if we really have to.'

'When Anne and I see him,' Katie said, 'we always say hello, but he just blanks us.'

'That's cos he doesn't know yer,' Faye said. 'He's wary of strangers. When we first moved in it took us ages to get a smile from him.'

'He and Faye are the best of friends,' Jo said. 'He prattles away in his language and Faye in English and if that fails they use sign language. Mind you, he scared you one day, didn't he, Faye? Remember when he was coming in, carrying a load of shopping. He was struggling and Faye went to take a bag off him. He got all agitated and snatched them back. After that he kept his shopping close to his chest when he saw Faye.

'Mrs Lowe said they starved 'em in the camps, that's why he's so possessive of his food.'

'He must have thought you were after his bottles of whisky Faye.'

'Ooh, what a thing to say, Dougie, that's out of order,' Tania said.

'Just wait 'til you want a ciggie off me,' Faye said.

'Only kidding, Faye,' he said. 'Will you accept my apology?'

'Nah, not unless you get on your knees,' Faye said.

'Bloody hell, I'm not that desperate, Faye.'

'You will be,' she said. 'Knowing you.'

We sat there on the stairs until the screaming had subsided and daylight was peeking through the skylight window. I was almost falling asleep. 'We'd better get to bed,' I said.

DOUGIE'S IN TROUBLE

I get back from work and see a police car parked outside the house. The front door is wide open.

Mrs Lowe won't be pleased, I'm thinking.

I go inside. The ginger cop is coming out of Dougie's bedsit. 'Hello, have you seen Dougie?' he asks.

'No, I haven't,' I say. 'Not since yesterday.' It was the truth.

'How's the job going?'

'It's OK,' I say.

'See many pictures?'

How did he know where I was working?

'It makes a change for someone to be working in this house,' the older officer says, as he comes out of the bedsit.

'You and your friend don't belong here. You can find a more respectable place than this.'

'No one bothers us.'

'You'll get sucked into all the crap, mixing with this lot. Have you got a boyfriend?'

I wanted to tell him it was none of his business, but thought I better not.

'No I haven't.'

'Ginger's a decent lad.'

Is he trying to get me fixed up with ginger?

Ginger blushes and grins at me as he makes his way out the door.

'His name's Jimmy. He's a nice lad.'

'That policeman is trying to get me fixed up with the ginger cop,' I say to Faye. 'How did he know where I was working?'

'He asked about you.'

'Did he?

'Yes, he's very interested in you,' Jo says. 'Do you fancy him?'

'No, not really. Imagine going out with a policeman? I'd be frightened to put a foot wrong.'

'Why are they looking for Dougie, anyway?' I ask.

'There's been another warehouse break-in,' Faye says.

'Now, you're not hiding anything in the ottoman, are you? Otherwise I'll have to report you to my new boyfriend.'

TANIA

'Tania's in the hospital,' Faye said. 'She's been beaten up by one of the punters.'

'Oh my God, is she alright?' I asked.

'Well, she's got concussion and broken bones, but they reckon if that friend of hers hadn't heard her screaming she'd have been dead. The guy who done it is a nutter. That woman who she rents her place from told me. She'd come to Tania's bedsit to pick up a few things for her. Tania had asked her to tell us. That's how we found out.'

Faye had knocked on my door. She and Jo were going to the hospital during visiting hours to see her.

'Do you and Katie wanna come with us?' she asked.

'Of course,' I said. 'I'll see if I can swap shifts at work. I'll need to pop to the village to telephone Marjorie. I'll just say that a friend has had an accident and has been taken to hospital. I'll meet you at the hospital.'

I took the bus to the Royal. When I arrived at the hospital I was told that Tania already had visitors and only two were allowed at the bedside. I had to wait outside the door. Faye saw me and beckoned me in. I shrugged my shoulders and mouthed, 'I can't.' The nurse was watching me.

Faye came to the door. 'You go in,' she said.

I went into the ward and saw Jo sitting beside her bed. I got a shock when I saw Tania. She had two black eyes and her face was swollen and bruised. Her

149

arm was broken and in a sling. It was in such contrast
to the last time I'd seen her, all dolled up and happy.

'How are you?' I asked.

'Well, I'm still here,' she said. 'The bastard didn't
finish me off.'

'He came bloody close to it though,' Faye said
angrily.

'Have the police caught him?' I asked.

'No, I can't tell the police,' she said. 'I'd get done
for soliciting. I just told them I fell down the stairs.'

'Do they believe you?' I asked.

'Probably not,' Faye said, 'but there's not a lot they
can do if she doesn't put in a complaint.'

'So you're going to let him get away with it?' I
said. I was angry.

'The woman who rents me her place will get done
'an all, so there's not much I can do about it. I'll know
to avoid him the next time.'

'The next time,' I said. 'Surely you're not going to
go out and do it again? You could get killed.'

'Shush,' Jo said.

The woman in the next bed was listening. She
looked at us.

'She wants to get rid of that fella of hers,' she said.
'The bully! Fancy beating her up cos she wanted a
night out with girls.'

'Yeah, some fellas are right control freaks,' Faye
said.

Tania shrugged her shoulders.

She had been plying her trade and had been beaten
up by a new client. She always asked for the money up
front and he had paid her. Afterwards, he wanted the

money back and she was not giving it to him. He had gone berserk.

'You should always give in when you're in a situation like that,' Jo scolded her. 'I remember I was in a situation like that once and I had to talk my way out of it. He was a very strange man, I can tell you.'

'My boyfriend's coming to see us later,' Tania said. 'He wants me to move in with him. He's gonna look out for me.'

I didn't understand a boyfriend encouraging her to prostitute herself, if he was supposed to love her.

'He'll more likely be her pimp,' Faye said when we left the ward. 'Yes,' Jo agreed. 'It'll be out of the frying pan and into the fire,' she said.

STRANGEWAYS

The ventilation tower of Strangeways Prison could be seen for miles and it was not far from where we lived in Cheetham Hill. Faye had asked me if I would go with her to visit Dougie, as he had given her two visitor's passes. Jo was unable to make it as she had a client to meet. Katie had gone home for the weekend to visit relatives. I had never set foot inside a real prison, although I'd often thought that living in the orphanage had seemed like one. I was both curious and interested to know what life was like behind bars in a real prison.

I set off with Faye one Sunday afternoon to visit Dougie. He had got time for handling stolen goods. We arrived at the big imposing front door. Faye pressed hard on the door bell. We heard a jangling of keys and an unlocking of the latch. It reminded me of the nuns in Nazareth House, with their bunches of keys. The heavy door was opened by a prison officer who looked at us suspiciously. 'We've come to see one of the inmates,' Faye said as she showed him our visitor passes. He examined it.

'Come in,' he said. We stepped over the wooden step and into a courtyard. 'Stand over there so I can see you,' he added.

A man in a kiosk was watching us. 'Afternoon officer,' Faye said. He didn't reply.

'Please yourself,' she told him.

'Shush Faye, don't get us into trouble,' I said.

Another prison officer turned up. 'More visitors,' the man in the kiosk said.

'Follow me,' the prison officer said and he turned and marched across the courtyard.

Faye copied him in a Charlie Chaplin style. I was horrified. 'Behave yourself, Faye,' I whispered.

I looked around at the barred windows that surrounded us. Whether real, or imagined, I could feel hundreds of eyes on me. We were taken to another part of the prison. The prison officer stopped at a heavy wooden door and unlocked it. He stood back to allow us inside. We were taken into the visitor's waiting room. The walls were painted green and there were bars on the windows. Without saying a word the prison officer locked the door behind us.

Other visitors were in the room and there was a palpable buzz. There were mothers carrying babies while bored young children ran around.

'Why are there bars on the windows in the visitor's room?' I asked.

'That's so we can't break into the cells and free the prisoners,' Faye grinned. 'They've hanged loads of prisoners behind these walls. Albert were a regular here.'

I shivered. 'I wouldn't like to have been a regular in the pub that he ran. I wouldn't have been able to look at him, knowing what he did.'

Faye shrugged her shoulders. 'That's life and some of 'em deserved it.'

A prison officer came into the room. 'Good afternoon,' he said. 'Before we take you to the visitor's room there's rules and regulations to follow.'

153

He proceeded to tell us what we could and could not do.

'Anyone who breaks the rules will end up spending the night in a prison cell.'

I couldn't wait to get out of the place. I'd been in a prison all my life and I valued my freedom.

We followed the prison officer down a long passage and stopped at another wooden door.

Before entering we were searched by a female officer, then we were allowed into the room. All the while we were closely monitored by other prison officers. The prisoners sat at separate tables.

We could see Dougie, looking pale in his dark blue outfit and as usual puffing hard on a cigarette.

He grinned. 'Hi,' he said. 'Glad you could make it.'

We sat opposite him.

'What's it like in here then?' Faye asked.

'Bloody awful. I'm banged up twenty three hours and I'm sharing a cell with two other prisoners. I thought one had really cracked up the other day. 'What's that out there?' he said. This other guy and me came to the window. It were the *sun* he were talking about. I tell you, this place cracks you up.'

I looked around the room. Some of the inmates were not much older than me. They looked scared, while the old timers laughed and joked. A prison officer was standing there closely watching us all. I felt like a criminal for just being associated with a prisoner.

'Six bloody months I got,' Dougie spat. 'That solicitor of mine was fucking useless.'

'Well, you do have a long record,' Faye said. 'He must have asked the court to take that into consideration,' she laughed.

Dougie grinned. 'I think he did, the bastard. I wonder whose side he were on. How's things at the Den of Iniquity?'

'Well, Mrs Lowe's rented your bedsit out to a young couple.'

'That didn't take her long.'

'When she found out you'd got six months, that was it.'

'I'll be out in four months, though. What's she done with all me things?'

'They're with me and Jo. Mind, you didn't have much, did you? I thought I'd find a few goodies hidden under the mattress or summit.'

'She couldn't wait, after all I've done for her,' Dougie said.

'Me and Jo told her about you getting that candelabra back for her. That'll keep you in her good books.'

'What did she say?'

'Said she didn't think it was you who took it. She said you might be a thief but you've got principles.'

'Bloody 'ell, did she really say that about me?' He grinned. Faye nodded. 'I've got witnesses,' she said, looking at me. 'Didn't she, Anne?'

'Erm, yes, she did.' I tried to sound convincing.

'Tell her I send her a big kiss,' he grinned. 'I'll have to keep in with her. I'll be needing somewhere to live when I get out.'

'Tania got beaten up by a punter,' Faye said. 'She's just got out the hospital. You should have seen the state of her.'

'She's lucky to be alive,' I said.

Dougie shook his head. 'She wants to stop doing that. There's too many nutcases around and that don't include the ones in here that I have to put up with.'

'She's moving out of her bedsit she's going to live with her boyfriend in Moss Side. But she'll still be on the game,' Faye said.

'Ah, so she's got herself a pimp?'

'That's what we think.'

Dougie tutted. 'She's a silly lass,' he said.

'How do you spend your time, Dougie?' I asked. 'Do you read?'

'Nah, the books they have here are crap. I just eat and sleep. I'm bored out of me mind. You could do summit for me.'

'I'm not helping you to escape.'

He laughed. 'Nah, can you send us in some of those girly magazines?'

'Girly magazines?'

'I can't go in the shop and buy them. I'll be embarrassed. If Faye gets them, I'll post them to you.'

'The prison officers read all the post before we get it. But I'll get it eventually.'

Soon it was time to leave. We said our goodbyes and left Dougie puffing hard on a cigarette, a resigned look on his face.

'Ah, its shame,' I said to Faye when we got on the outside.

'Ah, it's like a second home for Dougie,' she said. 'He can do the time no bother.'

ENDINGS

I finished with Colin. Our relationship was going nowhere, and it was unkind to lead him on. I told him that I wasn't ready to settle down. Katie's relationship with Jeff had also cooled since she returned from her visit to the North East. She had met up with her old boyfriend and was now feeling unsettled living in Manchester.

'Jeff's invited me to his mate's, they're having a party,' Katie said, 'but I don't fancy going on my own. He has some weird friends.'

I was content to stay in the bedsit and watch television but she pleaded with me to go with her. Reluctantly, I agreed.

We arrived at a house. Jeff knocked on the door. It was opened by a young lass who was heavily pregnant. She invited us inside. Loud music was playing. In the front room there were young lads and lasses sitting about. I'd no sooner sat down when a guy handed me a drink. I sniffed the glass. I was wary, especially since the El Dorado incident. 'I'll just have a can of lager this time,' Katie said.

A scruffy young lad came in with a packet of pills. He started sharing them out. One lad took a handful and popped them into his mouth. I couldn't believe it. 'What are those and where did you get them from?' I asked.

'Shush, don't ask him that,' Jeff said. 'He's probably nicked 'em from a chemist.' I was appalled. Jeff laughed.

'He shouldn't have that many, but he'll just sleep it off,' he said.

'Why do you need to take them?' I asked.

'They're happy pills,' he said. *Happy pills, who needs them?* I was getting high on life. I was young and I could do anything I wanted. Most importantly, I was free from the constraints of being a 'Nazzie House Girl'.

'Want some?' the young scruffy lad asked. Katie and I declined. Jeff took a couple of pills and popped them in his mouth. As the afternoon wore on people were giggling and talking gobbledygook. Even Jeff was being silly, laughing hysterically for no reason.

I was bored and I got up to go home. Katie told Jeff she was going to the loo, but we made our way down the hallway and out of the front door. I don't think he'd even realised we'd gone. People are not always what they seem. The following weekend Katie went back home to the North East. She met up with her old flame and they got back together.

She came back to collect her things and asked me to pick up her wages for her and put it towards the rent. Although I was sad that she was leaving I was happy for her. I took the opportunity to ask Janice if she would like to share a bedsit. She was delighted but we decided to look for a bedsit in another area. It wasn't long before we found one in a nice area of Crumpsall. We would be moving in after Christmas. First, I decided to visit mother in Liverpool.

MOTHER

The train arrives at Liverpool's Lime Street station. I see my mother waiting for me as the train screeches to a halt. Now that I have left the orphanage I am hoping to get to know her better. This is the reason I have contacted her.

I get off the train and make my way towards her carrying my small suitcase. She is scanning the people in the coaches. I catch up to her and tap her on the back. She turns around. 'Oh, you've changed,' she says. Since I last saw her at my sister's wedding four months ago I have dyed my hair blonde and it is held back from my face with a black velvet band. I am being scrutinised but I know that she is pleased to see me.

She suggests that we go to the pub first and have a drink. We find one not far from the station. I order a Babycham and Mother has a gin and tonic.

'This is my daughter,' she says to the barman. 'Isn't she lovely?' He looks over and smiles.

'Yes, she's very nice,' he says. I blush bright red.

'What long eyelashes you have,' she says.

'I think it's the mascara that lengthens them,' I reply.

We sit down.

'Where are you living in Manchester?' she asks.

'Me and Katie have got a bedsit in Cheetham Hill,' I tell her.

'Is that a good area? Do you feel safe living there?' she says.

'Yes, it's fine,' I reply. I don't mention the other tenants.

'You know,' she is saying in her Scottish accent, 'I didna want you to go to Manchester with that Katie. She's a bad influence, the way she just upped and left the North East, dragging you along with her.'

'She didn't force me to go with her,' I say, 'I wanted to. I can always go back if I don't like it.'

'Have you got a job?' she asks.

'Yes, I'm working as an usherette,' I say.

She screws up her face. 'You can do better than that,' she says.

'It's only a temporary job. I'm looking for office work,' I reply and she nods her approval.

'That band that you have in your hair,' she says, 'it reminds me of a song. It's called *The Black Velvet Band.*

'The song is very popular here in Liverpool, isn't it?' she shouts over to the barman. He has been listening to our conversation.

'It's on the music player,' he says.

Mother takes a sixpence out of her purse, goes over to the jukebox and drops it in the slot. The record drops and the music starts.

She sings along to the chorus.

Her eyes they shone like diamonds, they call her the queen of the land, and her hair hung over her shoulder, tied up with a black velvet band.

She seems happy. I'm glad that I came.

Mother wants to stay for another drink so I go over to the bar and order a Babycham and a gin and tonic. The pub is filling up with the regulars. We are sat near the door. She is relaxed and friendly. She smiles at the customers. 'Nice day,' she says.

A middle aged man walks in with a woman on his arm.

'I bet that's his fancy woman,' she says. 'I can tell. He wouldn't be bringing his wife out for a drink at this hour.'

I hadn't eaten anything that morning and was starting to feel the effects of the alcohol on my stomach. Mother went to the bar and came back with two packets of peanuts.

'Jimmy will have gone to the pub now,' she said. 'Let's go home.'

Jimmy was her long-term partner. He was in his late fifties. I didn't know where she'd met him but one summer when my sister and I came to visit her during the holidays he was there and had been a permanent fixture ever since.

All we knew was that he had been a merchant seaman. He'd had an accident for which he had been compensated and he walked with a limp. Elizabeth and I would have felt sorry for him but he resented us being there and would disappear to the pub whenever we were around. This would have suited us but he could be quite nasty when he'd had a skinful, or he would just sit in the armchair staring out of the window. We thought him very unsociable.

It was raining when we left the pub and we sheltered under Mother's enormous umbrella, which she often carried around with her regardless of the weather. I suspect she kept it as a weapon in case she was robbed. She was very security conscious and it made me wonder if she'd had a bad experience in the past. She had shown Elizabeth and me self-defence moves and advised us what to do if we were ever attacked.

We got on a green bus to Wavertree. There was no room downstairs so we climbed up to the top deck. We were enveloped in a fog of cigarette smoke and the smell of rain-drenched clothes. We sat at the front of the bus where we had a good view of the city. The rain made everything dull and grey. Mother pointed out places of interest as the bus moved along. I didn't take much notice. She told me we were on Penny Lane. The Beatles were to make a song about it.

We got off the bus near Wavertree Park. My sister and I had spent many a happy hour there when we had visited Mother in the summer holidays. We had taken photographs of each other in the lovely Botanic Gardens. Mother had a flat in Botanic Road then, which overlooked the park but now she rented a dingy two bed roomed terraced house in Cadogan Street.

We arrived at her house and she put a key in the lock and opened the door. We were greeted by the smell of stale cigarettes and musty carpets. There were two sitting rooms and we went through to the back one which was nearest the kitchen. There were half filled cups of tea on the coffee table and the ashtrays needed emptying. Mother didn't smoke so I presumed that these were Jimmy's.

'Sit down,' she said as she moved magazines from the two-seater settee. 'I'll put the kettle on.'

The door to the tiny kitchen was open. The sink was full of unwashed crockery. Mother had spent her formative years growing up in India and had servants to wait on her so housework was not her forte. I looked around the room. The once yellow wallpaper had faded and the pattern had long disappeared. Grey net curtains covered the window, which looked out onto the backyard. There was a wireless set on an old fashioned sideboard and mother switched it on.

The song *On the Street Where You Live* was playing. It was one of Mother's favourite tunes.

'I have often walked down this street before,' she sang.

I wondered if this song had any significance for her. Maybe she was remembering something from her past. I sat there bemused and in silence as she sang along.

'You like this song,' she nodded.

'I like the Beatles,' I said and asked her if she could show me where they lived.

'Ringo comes from the Dingle,' she replied. 'It's quite a poor area compared to where John Lennon lives. And every time he opens his front door he's besieged by fans.'

She had a soft spot for George Harrison. 'Those big brown eyes, and that mop of hair,' she said.

'Yes, the place is buzzing with their success,' she continued. 'Scotland Road is where Cilla Black lives. Her real name is Pricilla White. Her mother has a stall on the market. I often go there myself.' I was fascinated by all this information.

Mother loved Liverpool and had lived there for over ten years. She had made friends with the locals and would often stop for a chat on her way home from the shops. She knew all the shop assistants by name.

'How are you, May?' they would ask and she would enquire after their families.

'This is my daughter,' she said as she proudly introduced me in her Glaswegian accent. Some of them were curious as to why I didn't have a Scottish accent. 'She was brought up in England,' Mother explained. 'My other daughter, Elizabeth, has my colouring,' she would say, 'and she looks like Bette Davis.' I didn't think that my sister would have agreed with her.

I was getting to know Mother a little more. Now that I was grown up our relationship was changing. Before she had thought Elizabeth and I were impinging on her time and she struggled to feed us in the summer holidays. We never asked why we were put in Nazareth House, as it was a sore subject. When I tactfully approached the subject she'd just shrug her shoulders. 'Raphy put you in there,' she'd say.

Mother was very sociable and often conversed with total strangers. She was not averse to giving her opinion, whether they wanted it or not. On one occasion my sister and I were waiting to cross the road. The traffic lights turned to green and we went to cross the road. A lorry driver did not stop and went through a red light but realising his error he quickly slammed the brakes on. Luckily nobody was hurt but mother gave him a right rollicking. 'That was your fault,' she shouted, waving her umbrella at the red-faced driver. Elizabeth and I were mortified at the attention that she was drawing, but I suppose that she was just being assertive.

POVERTY

Wavertree had row upon row of terraced houses and the neighbours were in and out of each other's homes with the exception of Mother who never invited anyone back. Although Mother got on well with them I did wonder what they really thought of this well dressed woman, with her refined Scottish accent. She always dressed up, even if she was just going to the shops for groceries.

On our way back from the shops we would pass hordes of children of various ages playing in the street, some without shoes. The women would be standing on the doorstep with rollers in their hair chatting to their neighbours and catching up on the latest gossip. 'Hiya May,' they would shout. 'Is that the daughter? She looks a lot like you!' Sometimes they would invite us in for a cuppa. I loved the Liverpool accent and would sit there with mug in hand and listen as they exchanged humorous stories. One or other of the women had been beaten up and had bruised faces.

'What happened to her?' I would ask. Mother would just shrug her shoulders. 'That's life,' she would say.

One evening Mother said that she was going to visit a neighbour. She gathered a few of her and Jimmy's old clothes.

'This couple have four children,' she explained.

She told me that her neighbour's first husband had been an alcoholic. One night on his way home from the pub he had fallen over and banged his head on the pavement. He never regained consciousness and died in hospital the next day. His wife had since remarried but her new husband was also fond of the drink. They were living in dire poverty.

'If they offer you a cup of tea,' she said, 'just refuse because they need it themselves.'

The house was in an adjoining street. We went up some steps. The front door was dirty and bashed in as if someone had put their foot through it. Mother knocked on the door, which was answered by a woman in her thirties, although she may have been younger.

'Hello, May,' she said cheerfully. 'Come in, the kids are asleep, they're worn out.'

We followed her into the living room. Instead of the usual lounge furniture two bunk beds lay side by side in the middle of the room. In each of them lay two tousled fair-haired kiddies all fast asleep.

The pinstriped mattresses were dirty and there were no sheets on the bed. The bedding was a mixture of grey army blankets and coats and there were no pillows for their heads. There was no wallpaper on the walls and one bulb without a lampshade was hanging haphazardly from the ceiling.

I had never seen such poverty.

'We brought the beds downstairs,' the woman said. 'It's bloody freezing upstairs.'

It wasn't warm downstairs and I was wearing my coat.

'I've brought you a few things,' Mother said. 'There's an old suit of Jimmy's. It should fit Dave.'

'Ah, thanks May,' she said as she gratefully accepted the clothes. 'Can I get you a cuppa?' she asked in a low voice, fearful of waking the youngsters.

'No, thank you,' I answered, rather too quickly than I intended. 'We've just had one,' Mother said.

The front door was flung open. The woman's husband had arrived home from the pub.

'Shush,' his wife said. 'Don't you wake the little uns.'

He grinned. 'Shush,' he said. He had a round, cheery, red face.

'Hello May, is this your daughter?' he asked, looking at me through blood shot eyes. 'I hear you're training to be a nurse.'

This wasn't true, just one of the lies Mother would use to explain us not being around. Apparently she had told the neighbours that I was in a residential home training to be a children's nurse.

'I worked with children,' I said. That was the truth, albeit I was not training to be a nurse.

'That's a good profession,' he said. 'I like nurses, not bloody doctors though. Did you see Shirley Bassey on the telly, May?'

She had been the star of *Sunday Night at the Palladium.*

'I'll show you summit,' he said and went out of the room.

'Dave is daft on Shirley Bassey,' Mother said. 'He has all her records.' He came back into the room carrying a long-playing record. On the sleeve cover was the star looking glamorous in an ankle length glittering gown.

'Isn't she gorgeous?' he said, holding up the record sleeve. He kissed the picture. I couldn't help but think that the money he had spent on the record should have gone on the kids.

But his wife didn't seem to mind.

'He's smitten with her,' she said. 'I think he likes her better than me, May.'

'Well, she's better looking for a start,' he replied. His wife just grinned.

'See what I'm up against, May, and the kids daren't touch his records. He'd hit the roof if anything happened to 'em,' she said.

'I'm sure you could be just as glamorous if you had her money,' Mother said, looking at the frumpy woman with straggly hair and two front teeth missing.

'Eh! They'd have to work a miracle on me,' she laughed.

In spite of the dire living conditions she was cheerful and upbeat and I presumed this was the glue that held the family together.

It was a dark and dismal night and it was raining heavily as we made our way back home.

'He thinks more of his record collection,' I said, 'than he does of those kids.'

'Ach, he's not a bad man,' she replied. 'Three of the kiddies are not his but he treats them as if they were. I've seen the way he is with them and they with him. He's awful fond of them and they call him dad.'

'But why doesn't he get a job?' I asked.

'He does have a job but he doesn't earn much and he's fond of the drink. They struggle to keep a roof over their heads. I suppose his Shirley Bassey record collection is a kind of escapism,' Mother said.

'What about his wife stuck in that hovel? She'd be better off without him,' I said.

'She's happy she's got a man to share the burden. It's just that when things are hard they have to sell things. Those children would be better off in a children's home,' she told me. 'They would not have to worry about where their next meal was coming from. At least you were always well fed in the home.'

'It's a terrible way to live,' I said. She shrugged her shoulders and replied, 'You know nothing about life. You have been cosseted by the nuns.'

That was true but since coming to live in Manchester, I was learning fast.

ELLESMERE PORT

Mother had been invited to spend the weekend with friends in Ellesmere Port. They wanted to meet me so she had arranged a time when I would be in Liverpool. We caught a bus from Wavertree to the Pier Head. There was a queue waiting to board the ferry that would take us across the water. Mother bought two return tickets. Soon we were on our way.

As we sailed further from the Pier Head I thought of the song *Ferry Across the Mersey,* which was sung by the popular Liverpudlian group *Gerry and the Pacemakers.* The trip also reminded me of the time when I and some other girls had run away from Nazareth House. We had crossed the River Tees on the Transporter Bridge on our way to Hartlepool. It was the first time that I had been on it. I remembered the mixture of excitement and fear that I felt. It had seemed like one big adventure but I was fearful of what punishment we would receive from the nuns when we were found. I didn't doubt that we'd be caught and returned to the orphanage, but it had been fun while it lasted.

As the ferry sailed across to Ellesmere Port I watched the light glistening on the water as the squawking seagulls circled around us. There was a familiar scent of carbolic soap. I thought that I was imagining it. It was the soap that we had used in the orphanage. 'Can you smell soap?' I asked mother.

'Oh yes, that is coming from the soap factory in Port Sunlight,' she told me.

'Port Sunlight? What a nice name,' I replied.

We embarked at Ellesmere Port and got on the bus that took us to a new housing estate.

'This is it,' Mother said as we stopped outside a large semi detached house. It looked really posh. There was a neat garden with flowerbeds at the front. There was even a garage with a car parked in the driveway. *Such luxury!* We arrived on the doorstep and Mother rang the sparkling, polished bell. A smartly dressed woman in her fifties opened the door. She seemed genuinely pleased to see us. 'Hello Cecilia,' Mother said. 'This is my daughter.'

'So, you are Anne,' she said. 'I'm pleased to meet you. We've heard so much about you.' What could Mother have possibly told her? I bet she hadn't mentioned that I spent thirteen years in an orphanage. I hoped she wouldn't ask too many questions.

'Come in, it's lovely to see you,' Cecilia said as she held the door open for us. We went inside. There was a narrow plastic carpet protector in the hallway. Mother quickly slipped out of her high heels. 'Take your shoes off,' she whispered. 'We don't want to spoil the carpet.'

We followed the woman into the front room. My feet sunk into the plush cream carpet. There was a vase of hyacinths on the coffee table. The scent from the flowers transported me back to the May Processions that were held in Nazareth House. It was a sweet sickly aroma. 'Oh, they're lovely,' Mother said.

'Sit down,' Cecilia said. 'Make yourselves at home.'

At home? I'd never had a home like this.

'I'll just go and put the kettle on,' she said.

I looked around the room. There was a glass cabinet displaying delicate ornaments.

A large picture depicting a country scene hung on the wall above the fireside. The fireside itself was gleaming with matching gold accessories. Mother only had an old poker for hers. *Where had she met this woman?*

Cecilia came back in the room carrying a silver tray with dainty china cups and saucers that had pink roses painted on them. On a matching plate were various sandwiches without the crusts.

'Don't break anything,' Mother whispered when the woman had left the room. Somehow I much preferred the chipped mugs of tea offered by the neighbours in Wavertree. It wouldn't have cost a fortune to replace them. Mother seemed comfortable in these surroundings but I was on edge. She had spent many of her formative years in India. Grandfather had been a foreman in a steel foundry and at home they'd had servants to wait on them hand and foot. No wonder she felt at ease in this house.

There was a photograph of a smiling young lad in a royal navy uniform. He looked happy and proud.

'That's John, Cecilia's son,' Mother said. 'He's in the navy. He's coming home on leave tomorrow.'

'Will we have to leave then?' I asked. 'She won't have enough room for us all.'

'Of course she will,' Mother replied. 'This is a four bed roomed house. John hasn't got a girlfriend but his best friend has and we thought that you could keep him company. Just remember to tell him you're a nurse.'

I sighed. Oh no, I thought, not another blind date.

'But, I'm only an usherette,' I protested.

'But, you have worked in a nursery,' she replied.

So that's the reason I'm here, I thought, to be paired off with a young lad on home leave.

After a tense lunch, as I was more concerned about dropping crumbs on the carpet, Cecilia showed us to our rooms. Mother and I would be sharing a room with a double bed. We were provided with bathroom robes, soft white fluffy towels and comfy flip-flop slippers.

Cecilia's husband worked in the Vauxhall car factory. All was quiet until he bounced in the door. He was down to earth and such a contrast to his wife who was all airs and graces. He was passionate about politics and football and would voice his opinion to anyone willing to listen. Mother would nod indulgently as he ranted on about the injustice of it all. Cecilia would frequently remind him to keep his views to himself. 'We have guests,' she would remind him. 'Don't bore them.' I quite liked him. He was funny. I thought he looked like Clark Gable with his moustache and cheeky smile. Mother had told me that he'd had an affair in the past and warned me not to ask too many questions. It was still a sore subject between them, she had said.

The next day John travelled up from Portsmouth with his friend Peter. They had been friends from infant school and had enlisted in the Navy together. I was introduced to John, who was six foot four and towered above me. I was just five foot five.

174

He was taller than both of his parents. 'Maybe the genes skipped a generation,' Mother said.

Cecilia looked up at him, her face beaming. It had been months since she'd last seen him. 'Isn't he handsome?' she said. I really didn't want to go out with him. I felt shy and awkward but I couldn't say that to Cecilia.

'She'll be horrified if you refuse to go,' Mother had said. 'It will seem ungrateful.'

So, reluctantly, I had agreed to make up a foursome.

That afternoon I went out with him, Peter and Barbara, his fiancée. John put his arm around me and I thought he was too familiar. I felt embarrassed walking along with him in his uniform. I suppose some girls might not have minded but I didn't want the attention. We strolled around the park. Peter and his fiancée Barbara were obviously very happy together. They too had known each other from childhood. I felt like a fish out of water. They were talking about all things nautical. We had nothing in common and worst of all they'd been told that I was a nurse. I was asked all sorts of medical questions, which I couldn't answer. I don't know what they thought but we just made polite conversation after that. I was bored and couldn't wait to get back to Manchester. I promised that I would write to him but I knew in my heart that I wouldn't.

'What did you think of him?' Mother asked. She was keen for us to become a couple.

'He's a nice lad, but I don't fancy him,' I said.

She was disappointed. 'But he's tall and handsome and has such wonderful manners,' she replied. 'All the nice girls love a sailor.'

Not this one.

We boarded the ferry to Liverpool. Back in Wavertree Jimmy was waiting for us. He was grumpy, as usual resenting the time Mother had spent with me. She wanted me to stay and live with her. 'You could apply for a job at Littlewoods Pools,' she said. But I knew that it wouldn't work out and certainly not with Jimmy living there. She was disappointed but said she would come with me to Lime Street station.

As we waited for the train to arrive to take me back to Manchester we talked about Liverpool. 'It has two cathedrals,' she said, 'a Catholic and a Protestant one. And look at all the famous people that were born here and everyone is so friendly.' She would have done well working for the Tourist Board. I asked her if she would ever go back to Glasgow. 'This is my home now,' she said. I wasn't convinced. I wondered if there was a reason Mother couldn't go back there.

Mother told me about a prostitute named Maggie May, who used to ply her trade up and down Lime Street in the old days. There's a song dedicated to her and much to my amusement she started singing it.

Oh Maggie Maggie May, they have taken her away, and she won't walk down Lime Street anymore

The Manchester bound train arrived. 'Look after yourself,' Mother said as I boarded it. She waved and then waited until the train pulled away from the station. I looked out of the window and watched her standing there, a solitary figure on the platform, as she faded into the distance. I realised then just how lonely she was and I despaired at my broken family. I arrived back in Manchester with a mixture of emotions.

SAD TIMES

I sensed something was wrong as soon as I stepped in the front door. The house was unusually quiet. I carried my suitcase up the stairs. There was no music coming from the upper floor. There was not the usual chatter coming from any of the other bedsits. I unlocked the door to my bedsit and went inside. The room smelt of damp. I hadn't noticed it before, or maybe I had become immune to it. I sat down on the bed. I felt lonely. I wished Katie had been here but I was happy that she had made it up with her boyfriend and had decided to stay in the North East. I would not be staying here, anyway. Janice and I had found a nice bedsit in Crumpsall and we were going to move in there in the New Year. I was going to travel back to the North East to spend Christmas with my sister.

It was very cold. I looked in my purse but I had no coins to put in the meter. I would pop into Faye and Jo's bedsit, where I would be guaranteed a nice hot cup of tea. I knocked on the door of their bedsit. There was no answer. I wondered where they could be. I was just about to knock on Tania's bedsit but then I remembered that she had moved out a week before I had gone to Liverpool. Disappointed, I went back into my bedsit.

I consoled myself with the thought that Faye and Jo would soon be back and I'd catch up on all the gossip. I switched my transistor radio on. *Rocking Around the Christmas Tree* by Brenda Lee was playing.

I put my suitcase on Katie's bed, opened it and tipped the contents out. I'd need to take my clothes to the laundrette.

I heard footsteps coming up the path. I went to the window hoping to see a familiar face but it was a woman I'd never seen before. She came in the front door and I heard her walking up the stairs. I wondered where she was going. She stopped at Tania's bedsit. I could hear her humming to herself. I decided to introduce myself. I opened my door. 'Hello,' I said. She'd had her back to me. Startled, she turned round.

'Bloody 'ell,' she said. 'You gave me a fright.'

'I'm Anne,' I said. 'I've been away for two weeks. When did you move in?'

'Nearly two weeks ago.'

'It's so quiet,' I said. 'I'm not used to it. There's always someone about. Have you met Faye and Jo? They live in number five.'

'Oh, yes,' she said. 'That Faye came in the other night. She was the worst for wear. I had to help her up the stairs.'

That's not like Faye, I thought, she can usually handle her drink. I hope she hasn't fallen out with Jo.

'I've moved in at a bad time,' the woman said. 'Everyone was upset, even the landlady. They'd just heard one of the tenants had died.'

'One of the tenants *in this house?*' I asked.

'Yeah, she said he lived upstairs.'

I was shocked. Liam's away, so it can't be him, I thought.

'Was it the old man?' I asked.

'Oh no, it was a young lad. He committed suicide.'

179

I wasn't quite sure I heard what she was saying. I had to get her to repeat it.

'Did you know him?' she asked.

'Yeah, he was a nice lad,' I said, 'a really nice lad.'

'It must have been terrible for his family,' she said. 'Come in and have a cuppa, you've had a shock.'

I wanted to be alone, to think about what she'd just told me.

'I'd love a cuppa,' I said, 'but just give me few minutes.'

'I'm sorry if I've upset you,' she said.

'You haven't, not you, but thanks for letting me know.'

I went back into my room and sat on my bed. Liam's dead? I couldn't believe it. I was numb with shock.

I didn't want to stay in this house any longer. I didn't want to be alone. I locked my door and went into her room.

PAINT IT BLACK

$\mathbf{A}$ dark cloud hung over the house. It just wasn't the same. When I came in from work there was no music playing and everyone seemed subdued. A young couple had moved into Dougie's bedsit and she was pregnant. They kept themselves to themselves. He was actually working, which was a rarity in that house. A middle aged man had moved into Scots Billy's bedsit. One morning he was coming out of his room as I was walking down the stairs. He said something to me, but I was in a world of my own and barely acknowledged him. Besides, he spent more time outside the house than he did in. As for the old man who'd had a bedsit next door to Liam, he just kept repeating his old neighbour's name every time he saw any of us. I felt sorry for him; after all he had lost his entire family in the concentration camps, and now this.

The woman who had moved into Tania's bedsit was called Brenda and she was canny enough but she was going through a divorcé and had her own problems. I was relieved that I was moving on. Sitting in my bedsit alone I was too numb to cry. It didn't seem right even to switch my transistor radio on. If any of the songs Liam used to play had come on the radio it would have reminded me of him and opened up a torrent of tears. I thought back to the tune that he'd been playing the first day Katie and I had arrived here - 'Paint it Black'. That song seemed to have a sad significance now.

Everyone at work sympathised when I told them. "He just got fed up of life," Norma said. "I pity the one who found him." "These homosexuals suffer a lot from depression," Marj said. "It's something to do with the way their brains are wired. They do seem to get depressed more than other people." Ethel did her best to console me. She gently tapped me on the shoulder. "Don't fret," she said. "He's at peace now." Janice lightened the mood by talking of plans for our new bedsit. She was enthusiastic. "Ooh, just think of the fun we'll have," she said. "I'll have the freedom to come and go as I wish."

"Why did he do it?" I must have asked Faye and Jo countless times. Faye would shrug her shoulders. "Who knows what pushed him over the edge this time," she'd say. "I bet that Robbie won't be bothered," I said. "Oh, but he is," Jo said. "He has taken it badly." Then I felt guilty about saying it. He will never get the chance to say sorry, I thought. I got up to leave. "Come here," Faye said. She put her arms around me and enveloped me in a bear hug. "Look after yourself," she said. "I love you, yer know." "Yes, we're very fond of you," Jo said. I blushed from head to toe. I walked out of the room unable to speak. It was the first time in my life anyone had told me that they loved me. I sat in my bedsit and sobbed my heart out.

THE CHURCH

It was a dark night and pouring with rain. I was making my way to the bus stop when I passed a Catholic church. I hadn't taken much notice of it before. I decided to take shelter from the rain and light a candle for Liam. The welcoming lights shone through the coloured stained glass windows. I pushed open the wooden doors and went inside. I dipped my fingers in the holy water font and made the sign of the cross. I guess old habits die hard. All was quiet and peaceful. A handful of people were on their knees, silently praying. I genuflected and made my way over to the candle stand. It was in front of the statue of Our Lady holding the body of the crucified Christ. I gazed up at her sad face, which seemed to reflect the sadness I was feeling myself.

I took a candle, lit it and knelt in front of the statue. I said a prayer for the dead that the nuns had taught us. *Eternal rest grant unto him O Lord.....* I knelt there for a while, warming my fingers on the heat from the candles and reflecting on my life. So much had happened in only a few months. I had grown closer to my mother and got to know her a little. I'd arrived in Manchester with little knowledge of life. I'd met people on the fringes of society. They'd become my friends and because of them I would leave with a more understanding and tolerant view that would sustain me throughout the years ahead.

Some people come into our lives and quickly go.

Some stay for a while and leave footprints on our hearts.
And we are never the same.

Other book by the author

What would you do if you discovered you had a long lost sister who had been adopted soon after birth?

Would you go looking for her?

This is the dilemma that Anne Fothergill and her sister Elizabeth face when they uncover their mother's secret after her death.

The baby's name is Eileen and the siblings make the decision to find her – but it is a search which is to take them thirty four years and to the other side of the world.

When all three sisters eventually meet they embark upon a journey of discovery. They walk in the footsteps of a mother none of them know much about, a mother who had abandoned them.

Should Anne and Elizabeth tell Eileen the truth about their mother and the circumstances surrounding her arrival into the world?

Finding Eileen wasn't the end, it was just the beginning. This is a true story.

Printed in Great Britain
by Amazon

27962044R00109